DRAWING

History and Technique

DRAWING
History and Technique

Heribert Hutter

16 hand-mounted color plates
57 photogravure plates
22 line illustrations

McGRAW-HILL BOOK COMPANY
New York · Toronto

TRANSLATED FROM THE GERMAN
Die Handzeichnung
by D. J. S. Thomson

GERMAN EDITION © 1966 BY ANTON SCHROLL & CO, VIENNA
THIS EDITION © 1968 BY THAMES AND HUDSON
LIBRARY OF CONGRESS CATALOG CARD NUMBER 68-16484
31545
PRINTED IN AUSTRIA

Contents

DRAWING is one of the most elementary of human activities. Its origins go back to the very beginning of recorded history and it has continued uninterrupted ever since. Drawing is a pursuit that is open to everyone; it requires no special training. As it makes no particular claims on time or on artistry, it is in fact practised by everyone. And yet, however 'primitive' this elementary and spontaneous urge to draw may be, it nevertheless represents a major spiritual achievement. It presupposes a considerable capacity for abstraction, an ability to reduce the three-dimensional environment to a line on a two-dimensional plane. Reversing this process, in other words identifying the environment from the drawing, is almost as great an achievement. This practical, manual and visual familiarity with the technique of drawing is essential to any value judgment of the artistic merit of a drawing.

Quite apart from the broad spectrum of artistic or pre-artistic drawing in general, drawing in the narrower sense is a formal artistic creation, a process which begins with the first, rough sketch and ends with the completed drawing. As an artist's medium for expressing and formulating his ideas, the drawing has a long history, in which it has undergone a fundamental transformation. Up to the end of the Middle Ages it had strong social and functional associations, which gave it its essentially ephemeral character. Since then it has gradually developed into an autonomous work of art with a purpose of its own, entitled, by virtue of its intrinsic value as a creative work, to claim the right not merely to survive and to be preserved but also, as a spontaneous, highly personal 'manuscript', to rank as vital documentary evidence of artistic creation. The artist's 'handwriting', in other words his own peculiar form of line drawing, is immediately recognizable to the experienced eye. Hence it is possible to attribute an unsigned drawing to a specific artist with a fair degree of certainty.

Artistic drawing goes back to the very beginning of artistic creation as such. The earliest examples, graffiti on domestic utensils and coloured sketches in cave-dwellings from the ice age (Lascaux, Altamira), show remarkable self-assurance in reducing natural life to the two dimensions of the draughtsman. In these pictures, most of which represent the animal world, the characteristic feature of each species is vividly presented and typical movements are clearly brought out. Yet even when one feels one can recognize the work of a particular artist in certain caves, these pictures cannot be said to have an identity of their own or to rank as 'works of art' in the modern sense. These drawings are works which served a magico-cultural purpose.

As art evolved, the high artistic and cultural aims of the two-dimensional artist were taken over by the painter. The draughtsman and the painter tended to complement one another. The sketch and the detailed drawing played varying roles in the overall artistic evolution of the picture; but primarily they served to give cohesion to the basic artistic conception. Pure line drawing also continued to be practised and valued throughout all phases of cultural development – this is apparent in the unbroken fluency and assurance of the lines themselves – but nevertheless fulfilled a secondary, utilitarian purpose. Drawing remained the basis of painting, both in the evolution of the individual painter and in the development of the individual work: with the completion of the work, the process of draughts-manship is also completed. Drawing, as the painter's medium for giving the picture its initial form, is the first stage in a wall painting and frequently also in book illustration and panel painting. The artist draws the picture he has in mind in the original size on the spot – in the case of murals this is usually the last but one layer of plaster, in 'easel-paintings' the primed panel, and at a later stage the canvas. He then corrects and changes his rough draft. But these preliminary drawings are merely one of the stages of the production process; as the painting nears completion, it becomes progressively, and also materially, overlaid. The wide-spread devastation of the last war brought a considerable number of these wall sketches – 'sinopias' – to light, fully vindicating Oertel's theory of the gradual development of the technique of wall painting: 'Drawing and painting were simply two different facets of one and the same process, leading, in material terms, to one and the same end result.'

By comparison with these rough drawings, whose utilitarian, functional role is at once apparent, the drawings designed as book illustrations, of which a fair number have been preserved from early antiquity onwards, may appear at first sight to be a free and independent form of expression. Illustrations of mythologi-cal, religious and scientific scripts, which followed the text closely, provided a constant pretext for drawing, for translating words into visual terms. But it would

ANONYMOUS (South German, 1136/37). *Scribe and illuminator at work.*
Pen on parchment, 337:285 mm. Kapitelbibliothek St Guy, Prague. MS A XXI/1, f, 153.
Genre scene in the style of the South German (Salzburg) scriptoria first half of twelfth century.
The scribe Hildebert chases a rat from his table. Before him is the writing desk supported by a
lion and bearing two ink horns and two pens. His apprentice Everwin holds a panel on his knees,
on which he is painting

be mistaken to imagine that this was a free and uninhibited 'transcription' of a picture. The illustrator took great care to make a faithful reproduction, for he was essentially a copyist who, once he had hit upon a basic design, repeated it as accurately as possible. This care and the interest of antiquarians who tried to preserve the oldest and best drawings as models – which means, in most cases, those dating back to antiquity or near it – had the effect of preventing the free evolution of individual styles. This tendency to conform to a pattern explains the comparatively large number of 'copies' in medieval art and the continuation of the practice for several centuries. However, 'copies' should not be taken to mean facsimiles in the modern sense of scrupulously faithful reproductions. At the same time formal allegiance frequently transcended the barriers of content; antique, in other words pagan, compositions were adapted to Christian themes and fresh scenes were often devised from parts of traditional pictures. This constant experimentation with the 'copying' of traditional patterns also goes far to explain the calligraphic self-assurance of these draughtsmen, 'the cultivated ease with which the medieval miniaturist could extemporize a well-balanced composition within a prescribed framework' (Degenhart).

There are fragments of papyrus with illustrations of ancient writings, which date back to early antiquity and show a firmness of line and sparse but precise detail that clearly indicates a fairly long tradition of pen-and-ink drawing (Ill. p. 10). At the end of the eighth or the beginning of the ninth century the *Psalter of Corbie* appeared at Amiens, with illuminated initials done in two colours with pen and ink which are remarkable for their clear outlines and ornate detail. In marked contrast are the illustrations of the *Utrecht Psalter*, the most important example of the draughtsman's art from the early Middle Ages. They were produced in Rheims around 820. They represent a very open, fluid style of drawing with short,

VILLARD DE HONNECOURT (active c.1240). *Sleeping disciple.*
Pen on parchment, 79:143 mm. Bibl. Nat., Paris.
Pattern drawing from a 'Bauhüttenbuch' (book of
working designs). The orthogonal projection of the
foreshortened figure with the calligraphic portrayal
of hair and drapery were standard practice for
illustration drawing, (glass) painting and sculpture

hook-like, rapid strokes which lend a remarkable vitality to the early antique
motifs and forms. This style of artistic presentation was taken up with particularly
fruitful results in England, and also influenced miniatures. It was also adopted in
brush drawings and continued well beyond the eleventh century.

Typological scripts such as the *Speculum humanae salvationis* and *Biblia pauperum*
account for a very substantial number of the medieval illustrators' drawings. As
the avowed aim was to keep picture and text as close together as possible and as
such manuscripts were clearly in great demand, these picture-cycles, wide-ranging
both in scope and in subject matter, called for a high degree of craftsmanship and
the most appropriate medium would seem to have been the pen-and-ink drawing.
Not infrequently writer and illustrator were one and the same, but in most of the
workshops, which were monastic in their austerity, there was a clear division of
labour which is depicted in many an inscription and illustration (Ill. p. 9).

Precise iconographic examples to be followed appear in the collected
drawings from individual studios and artists which became known as 'pattern
books'. They too, like the rough drawings, show a linear graphic process to which
colour can be added. In this case, however, the process was deliberately employed
in order to lay down basic patterns and thus provide the painter with a rich
repertoire of forms, on which he could draw freely and which he could use again
and again. It is their role half-way between stereotype model and copy that
gives most of these collections their reproductive and impersonal character.

As these collections of patterns were designed for immediate use – and many
of them were undoubtedly used widely – few have survived. Here again traditions
must have lasted longer and been more widely applied than the relatively few
surviving examples suggest. The earliest of its kind is to be found in the fragments
of a papyrus dating back to the Ptolemaic and Coptic periods, in other words to

II

the first century BC and the fourth to sixth centuries AD. And even from subsequent centuries only a few specimens have survived. These again bear the impersonal stamp of a style of drawing which is designed to serve as a model, which has no artistic ambitions but is solely concerned to give a formal presentation of style and content, and which for that reason is often short lived. Additions made at a later period, superimposed drawings and frequent alterations are an indication of the enormous extent to which such works were used by countless generations of artists. The most important of these is a pattern book in the Bibliothèque Nationale in Paris, clearly designated in the accompanying text as an instructive collection of various patterns for further use. The collection was started between 1230 and 1240 by the architect Villard de Honnecourt, who took it with him on his journeyman's travels as far as Hungary, and the work was then continued by two younger masters (Ill. p. 11).

Similarly the few medieval individual drawings which are still extant were not preserved as documents with an identity and value of their own but as practical reminders and models for further use. Most of them are more or less faithful copies, and the style is often a pointer to the original artist. The majority of the fifteenth-century Dutch drawings still extant, specimens of which are to be found in the Rotterdam, Florence or Vienna collections, are copies of this kind. Many were undoubtedly erased, especially in earlier centuries, immediately after they had been used, so that the parchment could be employed again. One proof of this is a drawing based on a Byzantine mosaic: the parchment was used as writing-paper and today forms part of the Vatican Codex Barb. lat. 144. Pattern drawings on wax, wood and slate tablets, which could be wiped or scraped clean, may have suffered the same fate. It is clear, in fact, that these essentially utilitarian pattern drawings were not regarded as individual artistic achievements worth preserving.

Like the copies which were made of recent or even contemporary works, copies of antique works were also a prominent feature of the fourteenth century. And for the first time nature studies found their way into pattern collections, especially in northern Italy, in Lombardy. But once again direct observation of

I ANTONIO PISANELLO (Pisa 1395–before 1455 Verona (?))
Costume studies. Pen-and-ink over metal-point preliminary drawing on parchment, watercolour. 260:175 mm. Musée Bonnat, Bayonne. Reproduction slightly reduced.
Pisanello's costume studies served as both rough drawings and pattern sheets; he also designed brocade patterns. In the calligraphically ornamented pen drawing, the decorated design of the material is picked out in colour. The lady's fashionable hair style and the gentlemen's hats recur in Pisanello's wall paintings

nature was immediately translated into the formal style of the period, which could be readily understood and adapted. This process can be clearly identified in the pattern-book of the Biblioteca Civica in Bergamo, which carries on one page the 'signature' of Giovanni de' Grassi. This is a very mixed collection of drawings of animals, birds, human figures, ornaments and an illuminated alphabet, which contains not only the rough drafts of some pictures, enabling one to follow the process of transposition, but also works which were created on the basis of various drawings in the pattern-book.

Gentile da Fabriano and Pisanello, probably the most important of the early Italian draughtsmen, also show signs of this strange dichotomy between the imitation and adoption of already established patterns on the one hand, and an independent, creative study on the other, based on subjective observation of nature. At least some of these studies, which today are scattered among various collections (Louvre, Paris; Ambrosiana, Milan; Chantilly; Oxford; Rotterdam; Albertina, Vienna), originally formed part of a sketchbook, which was started by Gentile and continued by Pisanello and several other artists *(Ill. 10)*. Here one finds the work of a wide variety of draughtsmen: highly traditional drawings in a concise and well-proven style; studies based on classical sculpture with an obvious effort to achieve anatomical accuracy; naturalistic drawings based on direct observation; and motion studies, also from life, which show a certain sense of adventure in their wealth of detail and in the minute observation of plastic values and light effects. Indeed not a few of these drawings, such as Pisanello's fashion-sketches in Bayonne, Oxford and Paris (Plate I), are study and pattern combined.

The increase in the number of single-sheet drawings, which began in the late fourteenth century, coincided with the emergence of the independent picture and with a growing appreciation of the drawing as a work of art. Many of these single-sheet drawings give the impression of having been produced for their own sake, as 'autonomous' works; they are not simply the first stage of a finished picture and cannot be traced back to a specific painting but are the spontaneous expression of a creative artist. Nevertheless these drawings must also have been produced with a practical purpose. The earliest examples so far discovered of drawings which can be described as autonomous in the artistic sense were found by Bernhard Degenhart in the wide margin of a Vatican Codex. They are, for the most part, heads of Madonnas, which bear no relation to the text and have a freer line than drawings based on a specific model or designed for instructive purpose. The variety of techniques employed, which was obviously deliberate – lead stylus, silverpoint, pen with various inks – suggest that these drawings were in fact executed in order to try out the various technical possibilities. Other examples, which at first sight appear to be self-contained drawings, are in fact variants, though with a greater freedom of style and with considerable artistic appeal, which set out to express monumental themes in a restricted format. Typical of these is the comparatively large drawing in the Louvre depicting, with a wealth of detail, the death, ascension and coronation of the Virgin Mary. This work, which is reminiscent in style of the *Parement de Narbonne* and which Grete Ring has suggested was the design for a painting on glass, is probably a compressed version of a cyclical wall painting, adapted to form a self-contained composition. Bordering on the autonomous drawing are many examples of the international 'soft style' around 1400, in which traditional forms, calligraphy and nature study were combined with artistocratic refinement. They have, however, so much in common that it is difficult to identify the work of any one centre (northern Italy, Paris, Burgundy, Prague).

The widespread identity of style, which is a feature of the court artists around 1400, becomes less and less marked in the drawings of the fifteenth century. The fundamental difference in outlook which existed for a long time between the countries north of the Alps and Italy was reflected more and more in the drawings: in the north there was a growing tendency to produce work which was self-contained in composition and individual in its appeal, whereas in the south the accent fell more and more on studies. In the north the professional tradition of the pattern-book continued: most Dutch and German drawings of the fifteenth century are anonymous works based on masters whose style is often recognizable; whereas in the south the handiwork of individual artists began to stand out. In the north the nature study was developing into a composition in its own right, whereas in the south the free sketch was emerging, specifically designed to clarify a composition or highlight this or that detail.

GOTTFRIED KELLER (Zurich 1819–90) *Grotesque figure blowing soap bubbles.* Pen. Zentralbibliothek, Zurich. Marginal scribble on the manuscript of a poem. Example of draughtsmanship without artistic aspirations

The tendency in the north to aim at pictorial supremacy, even in drawing, is further reflected in the development of prints. The leading engravers in the second half of the fifteenth century, such as Master ES *(Ill. 39)* or Martin Schongauer, are also outstanding draughtsmen. One is always tempted to wonder, when confronted with their drawings, whether they were not ultimately intended for engraving; this is always a possibility. Painters' drawings are also often completed works, which cannot be identified with certainty as preliminary drawings.

In Italy the new attitude to drawing as the first and most personal preoccupation with an idea and its artistic development was clearly reflected in theoretical writings.

Theory of Drawing

The medieval artists' handbooks, one specimen of which has been preserved in the *Schedula diversium artium* of Theophilus, who lived around 1100 in the Helmershausen monastery near Paderborn, were planned purely and simply as technical manuals for working craftsmen. Even Cennino Cennini still follows the same pattern in his *Libro dell'arte* around 1400. In the short introductory chapters on the theory of art, where he deals with the basic ingredients of art, he places drawing before colour. A painter's training, he argues, should begin with drawing under some specific 'discipline', based upon models, so that the artist, having benefited by traditional experience and regular practice, can then proceed to develop his own ideas. The idea that drawing is fundamental to art and must be practised daily by the artist was already current in antiquity and was therefore widely promoted in the theoretical writings of the Renaissance, which took as their main authority the *Naturalis historia* of Pliny the Elder and his observations and anecdotes about artists.

Ghiberti also considered drawing to be the basis and theory of painting and sculpture in the *Commentari* which he wrote around 1450; likewise Vasari in the *Lives of the Artists* which he compiled in 1568. It is important to remember, however, that in these writings the *disegno*, or drawing, may refer not only to the sketch or single-sheet drawing but also to the artistic idea it expressed. For those writers who favoured mannerism in art, drawing, apart from the exercise it gives the eye and hand, was above all the first expression of the creative imagination, a sketch which prepared the ground for artistic composition. The urge to make things visible which are not immediately susceptible to linear representation, to express subjective values in graphic terms – a conception which can again be found in ancient writings handed down by Pliny – led to extreme emphasis being placed on contours, through which expression and movement were to be communicated. In the middle of the fifteenth century this conception, which was particularly popular in Tuscany, was disputed by Alberti and Filarete. They regarded drawing as an almost mathematical circumscription of the object, the sole purpose of which was to lend shape and which therefore could not claim any intrinsic value. This contour line should be soft and almost invisible, an element which only becomes effective when combined with composition and colour and which can never stand by itself as a basis of art.

These two opposing views became the criteria by which the role and function of drawing were to be repeatedly judged in the centuries to come.

For Leonardo da Vinci, drawing was an almost scientific means of acquiring knowledge. He realizes that the line does not exist in nature, in other words that it is an intellectual abstraction with the help of which facts may be clarified but not fully reproduced. Hence the great importance he attaches to detailed studies and the compulsion he felt to move on from the drawing to the painting, to the picture.

The Venetian and Lombard artists and theoreticians also regarded drawing as a means of capturing an idea *(concetto)* quickly and preserving it in one of several established forms *(schizzi, abozzi)*. A practised eye is essential to the capturing of the idea, a practised hand essential to its expression in painting, and the drawing is merely an intermediary.

A striking feature of all these theories is the fact that they refer only to the act of drawing, or to the sketch or the study. The drawing as an aim in itself is never referred to and the noun in fact is never used except in Leonardo's scientific sketches. The Italian Renaissance drawing is 'unashamedly utilitarian' (Oertel).

This explains why the 'autonomous' drawing was so rare in the south. Even when, for example, portrait drawings bear the hallmarks of completed works, only in exceptional cases can they have been regarded as end products with a validity of their own. One such exception appears to be Michelangelo's large single-sheet drawings, particularly the so-called Cavalieri drawings, which bear no direct relation to works either executed or planned. In these presentation drawings, however, the highly personal character and the dedication in the 'signature', or handwriting, are the decisive factors. That such drawings were greatly valued and sought after is clear from Vasari's reports on Michelangelo's 'teste divine' (*cf.* Plate X).

Sketches were also regarded as 'signed' documents; this is conclusively proved by a sketch of Raphael's in the Vienna Albertina, which shows a study of a head and two nude figures in the Stanze of the Vatican and which bears the following inscrip-

17

tion by Dürer: '1515. Raffahell de Urbin, who was so highly regarded by the pope, has made this naked picture. And has sent it to Albrecht Dürer in Nuremberg, addressed by his own hand.'

Dürer himself, however, seems to have attached no intrinsic value to sketches as such. Although he was the outstanding draughtsman of his generation and had a decisive influence on the further development of German art in the sixteenth century, Dürer's theoretical writings expressed views on drawing as a form of art. In the completed sections of his *Speis für den Malerknaben* ('Meal for the painter's apprentice') he is mainly concerned with the didactic principles of perspective ('Instruction of Measurement', 1525) and the doctrine of proportion ('Four books of human proportions', 1528). For Dürer, to whom the concept of the *prima idea*, the artistic inspiration, was completely alien, the goal towards which he strives is the finished composition and precise execution. 'A good picture cannot be made without industry and effort.' At the same time by 'picture' he also meant the completion in pictorial terms of the composition for subsequent engraving. Drawing he regarded as something quite separate. If 'someone one day sketches something on paper with a pen, [that] is artistically another matter.'

The theoreticians of the sixteenth century were firmly committed to the two stages of the creative process: drawing as an idea, a mental picture, and drawing as a material visualization of the idea, which is clarified and finally captured in various forms.

Federigo Zuccari in his book *Idea de' Pittori, Scultori et Architetti*, which appeared in 1607, gave another interpretation of drawing. For Zuccari, who based himself on the neo-Platonic, universal principle, idea and drawing were identical. Anyone can produce an 'inner' drawing, a *concetto*. The 'external' drawing, the simple, linear contour of figures, is a product of this mental *concetto*. Under the influence of artistic imagination the drawing becomes more and more complex and capable of expressing all human inventions, fantasies and eccentricities, far beyond the various historical and poetic themes.

This universal conception ascribed to drawing, which until then was merely regarded as a means to an end, a material object, an intrinsic value and great importance. It was not just placed on a par

with other arts but in a certain sense valued even more highly. It is no coincidence that at this stage drawing began to arouse more and more interest. Drawings were now collected, classified and dedicated as individual works of art. The connoisseur and the art-dealer who had, of course, already made their appearance and had even shown occasional interest in drawings, achieved in the seventeenth century a position which they were to maintain for centuries.

By contrast with the over-subtle evaluation of drawing of the late mannerists, the theoreticians now became more concerned with the outward appearance. In the course of studying and evaluating the relationship between line and colour, they revived previous theories, improved upon them, compared them and constantly re-examined them. Vasari's theory of the formal priority of drawing over painting was recognized to be specifically Florentine and contrasted with the northern Italian conception of painting, which neglected line, and sought to abolish the contour. Passeri (*Vite de' pittori, scultori et architetti, che anno lavorato in Roma, morti dal 1641 fino al 1673*) believed that the ideal combination of these two extremes was achieved by the 'Roman school' and therefore attached particular value to the drawings of Raphael and his school and those of the baroque reformers, the Carraccis.

In the conflict between the 'painters' and the 'draughtsmen', which is one of basic principle and was by no means confined to sketches, the antagonists took up strongly entrenched positions, which gave rise to bitter controversies, especially in France, between the champions of colour, the Rubenists as they were called after their chief spokesman, and the Poussinists, the champions of drawing as the supreme artistic conception. In the academies the traditionalists gained a firm footing with their emphasis on drawing as a means to composition. Here, inevitably, more importance was attached to the practical side, to the instructive and didactic element. Textbooks laying down classical rules of form appeared in all parts of Europe. Drawing was again assigned the role of practice and preparation. But at the same time its value as primary evidence of the artistic personality was more and more widely acknowledged. In 1681, for example, Roger de Piles rated the 'esprit du contour' higher than the exact reproduction of nature, as one of the possible types of drawing, and also higher than the idealistic drawing, which to some extent improves upon nature. The spiritual and pictorial line, which he found at its most expressive in Rubens' drawings, gives 'the picture soul and has the effect of making the body appear to be really of flesh and to be full of blood and life'.

In the eighteenth century more and more authority was given to the judgment of the connoisseur and enthusiast. In *The Theory of Painting*, which appeared in 1715, Jonathan Richardson, father and son, consider the original importance, the intrinsic value of drawing to lie in the purely graphic lineament and the contrasts of light and shade, which make colour superfluous. They stress the pure originality of drawing and place it above painting. In 1741 Pierre-Jean Mariette produced his *Réflexions sur la manière de dessiner des principaux peintres*, in which he laid down criteria for the criticism of drawing which are to a large extent still valid. He left the artists to wrangle over the old question of whether drawing should take precedence over painting, but he himself was in no doubt that the verdict was for drawing: 'One single stroke with pen or charcoal answers the unspoken question that everyone is asking. Colour as such is incapable of doing this.' A. J. Dezallier d'Argenville also places drawing above painting (*Abrégé de la vie des plus fameux peintres*, 1745), for drawing, in his view, reveals the artist's genius most directly, whereas in painting he must adapt it, suppress it, subordinate it to a plan.

Although the importance of drawing as a personal document 'signed' by the artist was widely accepted and drawings became collectors' pieces, their formal and functional position remained in dispute. In periods dominated by a classical style the pure graphic, linear contour drawing with plastic values was widely appreciated, but for the most part it was regarded as no more than a form of exercise, a preparation. At other times, when painting was in vogue, the drawing was widely accepted as a work of art in its own right and frequently the sketch was rated higher than the completed work. Until well into the nineteenth century the academies clung to their conviction that drawing served only a subordinate function, but there was a general trend towards a more colourful, freer type of drawing which was also accepted as a work of art. Two artists, in particular, expressed views which

epitomized the dominant trend of the nineteenth century. Whereas Eugène Delacroix, at the beginning of the century, considered that the value of the sketch lay not in suppressing detail but in subordinating it to a strong line, Max Liebermann towards the end of the century described drawing as the 'art of omission'. Significant, too, was the increasing importance of colour, the development of wash drawing and watercolour. 'A drawing is merely the external circumscription of what we see', said Paul Cézanne in his conversations with Gasquet. He completely eliminated line from his work – yet he is one of the outstanding draughtsmen.

Line alone is no longer enough, it is 'purely a question of proportion,' declared Paul Klee, who looked to drawing to provide an opportunity for 'psychic improvisation'. This at once opens up entirely new fields and new functions for drawing. In the twentieth century drawing is achieving its independence by advancing from a form of reproduction and abstraction to what is in effect a highly personal statement. It acquires a value of its own in the fullest sense and constitutes an art-form *sui generis*.

Collectors' Marks

The custom of making a collector's mark on a drawing is almost as old as collecting itself. The earliest examples are to be found on drawings by Stefano da Verona in the fifteenth century (Lugt Collection, Paris). Vasari labelled and framed the drawings in his collection. Since the seventeenth century monograms, frequently combined with emblems, have been common usage (see 1 – 4 below).

(1) Charles de Ligne (1759–92), Lugt 592
(2) Albert Sachsen-Teschen (1738–1822), Lugt 174
(3) Pierre-Jean Mariette (1694–1774), Lugt 1852
(4) Jonathan Richardson the Elder (1665–1745), Lugt 2183

19

1 ALBRECHT DÜRER (Nuremberg 1471–1528)
Self-portrait. Silverpoint on white-grounded paper, 1484. 275:196 mm. Albertina, Vienna. Cat. IV, no. 301; Winkler 1. Reproduction in original size.
Both technically and artistically this drawing, the earliest still extant, done by the artist when he was not yet fourteen, shows astonishing maturity. Later Dürer himself inscribed it: 'This portrait of myself I made in a mirror in the year 1484 when I was still a child Albrecht Dürer.' The original position of the forefinger as it was drawn in the preliminary sketch, which could not be erased from the grounded paper, is clearly visible. In the purely linear silverpoint technique, shadows are produced by repeating lines and plastic curves by cross-hatching.

2 PIETER BRUEGEL THE ELDER
(Brueghel 1525/30–1569 Brussels)
The Yoke. Pen in dark and light-brown ink over black crayon, *c*. 1564. 164:184 mm. Albertina, Vienna. Cat. II, 811; Münz 81. Reproduction in original size.
Bruegel expressly described this drawing as a nature study (inscription below: nart leven). As the notes on colour details show, the artist's intention was eventually to produce a painting.

3 JAN ASSELIJN
(Dieppen near Amsterdam, *c*. 1610–52 Amsterdam)
Bent Vueghels. Brush in bistre with colour wash, 183:237 mm. Stiftung Preussischer Kulturbesitz, Kupferstichkabinett, Staatliche Museen, Berlin.
The Dutch painters living in Rome in the seventeenth century had formed a guild of their own, the 'Bent'. Unlike the native artists, they drew and painted from life. There is a certain irony in Asselijn's treatment of a group of his colleagues working in the open air, and the stylized inscription makes the work almost a form of personal reminiscence.

4 JOHANN ADAM KLEIN (Nuremberg 1792–1875 Munich)
The painter Ernst Welker on the Kapuzinerberg near Salzburg. Pencil, 1818. 197:229 mm. Privately owned.
The discoverers of the romantic sub-Alpine landscape in the early nineteenth century were concerned above all to reproduce the landscape with as much topographical precision as possible. With a sharp, hard pencil they recorded the particular, unique situation noting the day and even the hour.

5 ANTON VAN DYCK (Antwerp 1599–1641 London)
Portrait of Jan van Ravesteijn. Black chalk, 252:201 mm. Albertina, Vienna. Vey 265. Original size.

Van Dyck drew this portrait of the Dutch painter Jan van Ravesteijn on one of his prolonged visits to The Hague in 1628/29 or 1632 as one of a series of portraits of important contemporaries which he was planning. Van Dyck himself produced eighteen etchings in the *Iconographia* series of portraits. For the rest he had outstanding etchers at his disposal who were also capable of applying printing techniques to free and painterly portraits, as was done by Paulus Pontius in the case of this portrait.

6 SALVATOR ROSA
(Arnella near Naples 1615–73 Rome)
Garden gate in the park of the Villa Madama in Rome. Brush in bistre over a pencil sketch, traces of red ochre, 250:210 mm. Gabinetto Nazionale delle Stampe, Rome. Reproduction slightly reduced.
The areas of light and shade in the motif, which was chosen for its picturesque quality, are interwoven with incredibly lively effect by diluting or concentrating one colour.

7 WINSLOW HOMER
(Boston, Mass. 1836–1910 Scarboro, Maine)
The Last Boat In. Pencil, 209:305 mm. Andover, Mass. Addison Gallery of American Art.
Homer drew this scene from the hard and dangerous life of fishermen with complete realism, but injected a dramatic note by deliberately distorting the perspective and by accentuating the shadows.

8 ADOLPH MENZEL (Breslau 1815–1905 Berlin)
Workers in a steel rolling-mill. Pencil, 225:305 mm. Nationalgalerie, Staatliche Museen, Berlin (East).
The steel rolling-mill, which Menzel completed in 1875, was one of the first industrial pictures to be produced. In the preliminary sketches which he made for this picture he noted details of colour and light. That the artist was primarily interested in the optical impression is also clear from the drawing, in which certain details are omitted in order to give a coherent, overall impression.

9 GUSTAV KLIMT (Vienna 1862–1918)
Standing woman looking to the right. Pencil, 1917. 496:324 mm. Albertina, Vienna.
Klimt's drawings of moving figures are characterized by curving, relaxed lines which produce a rhythmic effect that is almost ornamental. Yet the individuality of the lines brings out both the surface and the volumes. Many of Klimt's studies look like independent drawings.

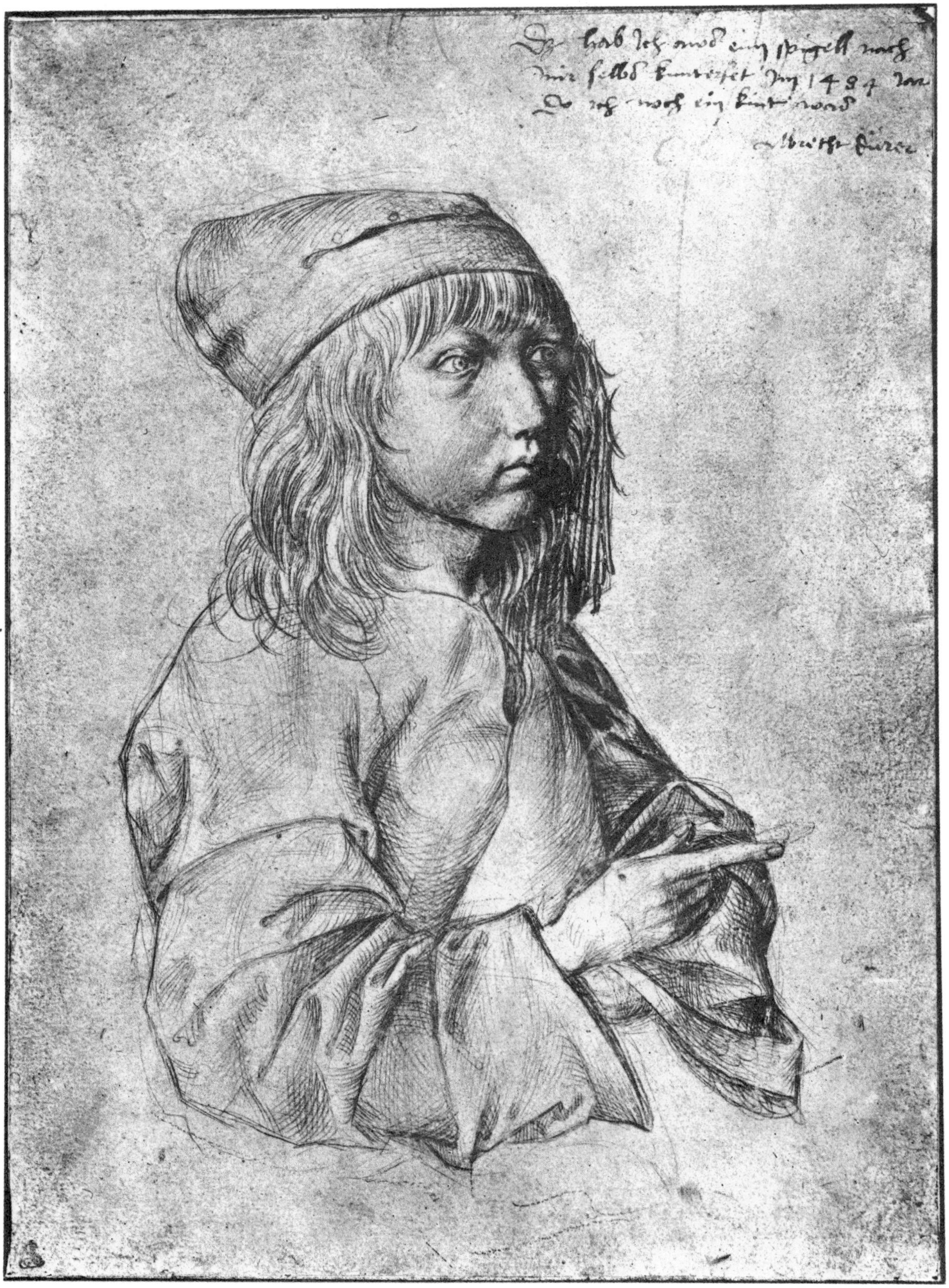

1

2

Bent Vrueghils.

3

4

SRosa · cancello Vicino villa madama

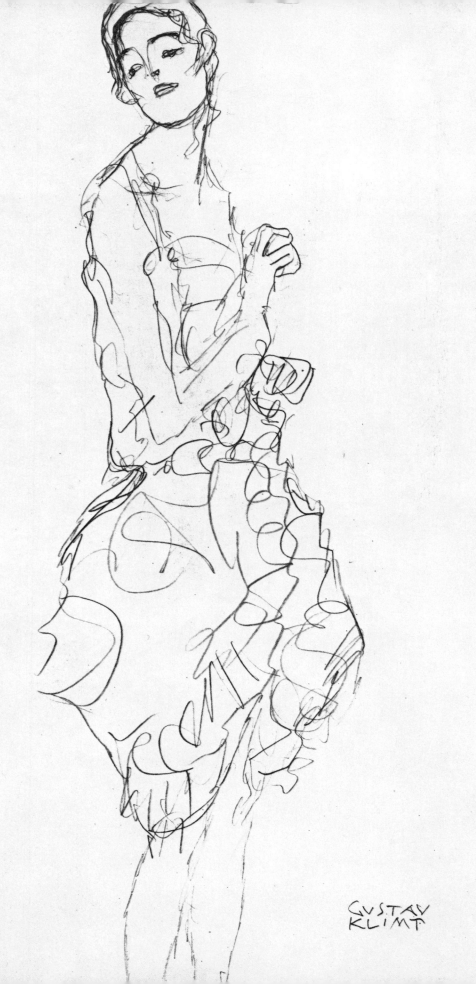

9

GVSTAV
KLIMT

The Functional Drawing

IT WAS NOT until the fifteenth century that drawings were preserved to any appreciable extent as individual sheets, but from then on the practice spread very quickly. As I have already pointed out, this does not mean that in earlier times draughtsmanship was a limited, much less non-existent, craft. Nor can one assume that a decisive factor was the growing production and popularity of cheaper paper, which replaced parchment more and more as a medium for writing and drawing. The developments which were primarily responsible for the enhanced prestige of the single sheet in particular and of drawing as a whole were undoubtedly the change that took place in the layman's view of pictures, which became more and more widely accepted as individual self-contained, detachable and indeed detached works of art, and the change that also took place in the public attitude to the process of artistic creation. And it was no coincidence that in the fifteenth century Italy was the main centre of individual draughtsmanship, not merely in terms of the number of artists who could be defined as draughtsmen but also in terms of the various types of drawing which were produced. It was here that the evolution from medieval theoretical thinking to the anthropocentric approach of the Renaissance began, and it completed its course far ahead of the rest of Europe. One inevitable effect of this immensely important historical process was a fresh evaluation of the artist and his work. Specific functions were allocated to drawing in the apprenticeship of artists, which was no longer organized purely in terms of handicraft. Drawing had an important part to play both in the artistic development of the apprentice and in the genesis of the individual work of art.

But drawing also had a legal role to play, for it provided a document on the basis of which contracts for public works were negotiated or competing designs considered. In the not infrequent contracts between artists and employers, most of whom were professional or communal bodies (the private patron made direct personal contact) the conditions laid down were often very strict and the drawing, the design, was completely binding. This particular function of draughtsmanship has, of course, persisted up to the present day, although the close approximation of the design to the finished work, which was still valid in the baroque period, has been relaxed to allow considerably more artistic licence.

Attempts have frequently been made to break down drawings into clearly defined categories, but any such attempt is bound to be somewhat arbitrary. The frontiers are almost always blurred and the outward appearance of a drawing is often no clear guide to its original purpose. In no branch of art history is criticism and classification so dependent upon an intensive, individual and unprejudiced study of the individual work. Here the tradition of connoisseurship is still very much alive and is an important criterion in many cases where decision is difficult.

By far the greater part of early drawings, and particularly those of the Italian Renaissance, was produced with a specific function and purpose in mind.

The workshop tradition gave rise to copies and studies. In the process of creating an artistic work in another material, usually for paintings but also for sculpture, architecture and handicrafts, preliminary drawings, studies in composition and detail, and 'cartoons' or working drawings in the original size were produced.

It is impossible to draw a clear dividing line between this large group of functional drawings and 'autonomous' drawings, which were not designed to serve a particular purpose but were solely or at least predominantly an expression of the creative urge and an end in themselves.

The Copy

The training of the artist began with drawing from a pattern. To begin with, there were the patterns which had been graphically reduced and reproduced in the flat, that is to say other drawings, pictures and – more and more important as time went on – engravings. The second most difficult stage was considered to be drawing from sculpture, the object being to express the three dimensions of the body by graphic means, by drawing lines on a flat surface. Here copying ancient reliefs and statues had a special role to play. Moreover the conventional ideal of antiquity could be directly copied from originals, genuine or otherwise, which had been recently discovered and were being closely studied. Drawing from nature came only in third place, but Cennini already regarded it as the culmination of artistic training: 'The most complete guide, the best pilot, the triumphal arch of drawing', is how he described it. But as a rule the term 'nature' did not mean the spatial dimensions of a landscape but the study of models in a studio.

II REMBRANDT HARMENSZ. VAN RIJN (Leiden 1606–69 Amsterdam)
Portrait of Baldassare Castiglione. Pen and brush in bistre, white relief, 1639. 163:207 mm. Albertina, Vienna. H. d. G. 8859; Benesch 451.
Sketch done from memory after seeing Raphael's picture, which was auctioned in 1639 in Amsterdam. The handwritten notes refer to the proceeds of the auction. The white highlights on shoulder and right arm oxydized black. Rembrandt employed Raphael's pose in his etched self-portrait of 1639

Copies are therefore of particular interest when they are more than mere exercises. Copies of important artists can provide significant clues to the draughtsman, partly in his choice of model, partly in the way he copies. It is seldom a straight reproduction but more of a paraphrase. Thus Dürer in his drawings adopted the classical ideal of the human figure from Mantegna's engravings and from drawings by Jacopo de Barbari and reproduced it in his own peculiar linear style. Michelangelo, in his drawings from certain of Masaccio's figures, emphasized the sculptural proportions of the human body, which had a special appeal for him as an artist with a strong tactile sense and which had been an innovation of great historical significance on the part of Masaccio a century before.

Baccio Bandinelli's drawings from ancient sculptures, in which he magnified the naturalistic muscular anatomy of the models, most of them Greek, and gave it added prominence by means of short, dynamic, unconnected curves, are no less significant as documentations of classical figures than as sixteenth-century drawings (Ill. 30). And they in their turn were regarded as models worth imitating.

Rubens was nothing if not methodical when, as an already acknowledged master and well provided with princely commissions, he travelled to Italy to make studies of the classical artists of the Renaissance and the painters of the generation immediately before. His Italian drawings, which are to be found today in many different collections, reflect the vast scope of his artistic interest, which ranged from ancient monuments to great compositions, from single figures to minute detail (Ill. 31).

In many instances a copy was made for purely personal reasons, as was the case with Rembrandt's quick sketch of a painting of Raphael's, which he made during an auction in Amsterdam in 1639 (Plate II). The inscription reveals his interest in the art market: above: 'de Conte batasar de Kastijlyone von rafael—verkooft voor 3500 Gulden'; below: 'het geheel caergesoen tot Luke van Nuffeelem—hefd gegolden f 59456:—: Ano 1639' (the entire cargo of Lucas van Nuffeelen fetched 59,456 Gulden). The fact that he adopted the same pose as in Raphael's picture in an etched self-portrait the same year shows how much he was influenced by the original portrait, which now hangs in the Louvre.

Frequently, too, artists copied their own works, either to retain the composition for further use in the event of a sale or to compile a sort of catalogue, which would serve to document the authenticity of the works. One of the most important collections of this kind is the *Liber veritatis* of Claude Gellée, known as Le Lorrain, which is in the British Museum in London.

Drawings of pictures which were produced in the studio of a well-known painter were made by the master himself and also by apprentices and students. Many such specimens which emerged from Rembrandt's workshop can be seen to have been corrected or 'gone over' by the master, in other words fairly large portions were redrawn and the detail considerably clarified. It is, therefore, often only possible to decide whether a particular drawing is an original or a copy, whether it was drawn by the artist himself or by someone else, by carefully comparing the style and the handwriting.

An interesting light is thrown on the relationship between model and copy if one compares a drawing by Titian *(Ill. 32)* with the copy by Watteau *(Ill. 33)*. Titian's picture of two kneeling boys in a landscape hangs today in the Albertina, Watteau's drawing in the Louvre. The changes made in what is on the whole quite a faithful copy are characteristic of the divergence of views of the sixteenth and eighteenth centuries. Watteau's picture comes even nearer to the square, and soft tones of red ochre have replaced the harder lines of the pen. The contrast between the large proportions of the figures in the foreground and the expanse of landscape in the background, which in Titian's picture were clearly drawn in two separate stages, is toned down by the evenness of the lines. Watteau's treatment is more coherent, more compact and more harmonious, but less exciting; it has all the sure, detached elegance of the drawings of the early eighteenth century.

The tendency to turn time and again to classical models, to antiquity as well as to the Renaissance and finally to the baroque reform around 1600, the 'austere' Roman baroque, had the effect, especially in the late eighteenth and early nineteenth centuries, in classicism and in the religious romanticism of the Nazarenes, of elevating the function of drawing from older models above the level of a mere didactic exercise. The ideal of clear compact contours and of a three-dimensional figure continued to influence the choice of models, and wherever possible was given prominence in the technique of copying. A personal signature seemed less important than the rules—whether real or imaginary—governing the composition of the model, rules which the artist had to comprehend.

In the course of the nineteenth century, copying an artistically set subject gave way more and more to individual and even arbitrary interpretation, and culminated eventually in the virtual abandonment of formal restraint in twentieth-century art. Despite his highly personal style and dramatic licence in his drawings, how comparatively close, for example, Vincent van Gogh is to his model, Millet; and how uninhibited is Picasso, on the other hand, when he paraphrases old and more recent masters such as Delacroix, Manet (Ill. p. 34) or Velazquez in his paintings and drawings. Copies of works which were subsequently lost or altered may be of little artistic importance, but their historical value is often immense. We owe our knowledge of the Calendar of 354 entirely to the copies made in the seventeenth century, and even they reveal that they were not based on the original but on a Carolingian copy. Similarly, to name only a few more examples, the

PABLO PICASSO (Malaga 1881) *Luncheon on the grass*. Pencil, 1961. 270:420 mm.
From a sketchbook with paraphrases of Manet's picture *Déjeuner sur l'herbe*.
Picasso has adapted the model composition, which goes back in part to one of Raphael's groups
of figures, to his personal smooth and flowing linear style in a highly subjective manner. Into
this 'copy' of Manet he introduces a novel atmosphere of antiquity with 'classical' profiles

original decoration of Santa Constanza in Rome has only survived in the drawings
made of it. Giotto's *Proclamation of the Year of Rejoicing 1300*, of which only the
centre-piece remains in the Benediction Loggia of the Church of the Lateran, has
been preserved in its entirety in a seventeenth-century drawing now in the
Biblioteca Ambrosiana in Milan; the famous *Navicella* by the same artist was copied
as early as the fifteenth century (New York, Metropolitan Museum) and can be
compared and checked with later copies. Even in the age of photography, drawings
of works which have been poorly preserved, are difficult of access or for other
reasons cannot be photographed, are often more revealing and more valuable
than mechanical reproductions. A good example of this are Wilpert's watercolour
reproductions of catacomb wall paintings, which for decades were the most
reliable guide in this important field.

Of inestimable value to classical archaeology are the drawings which were made
of ancient statues soon after they were discovered and before restoration work

began. In fact many works are only known to us from such drawings. The same is also true of architectural works.

Composition Sketches and Rough Drawings

Drawings which are made with a specific work in view invariably follow the same basic artistic progression, although naturally all the possible stages do not always occur in strict logical sequence or indeed occur at all. The individual artist's method of working is a constant imponderable. There have been many artists, Michelangelo da Caravaggio and Diego Velazquez among them, who did very few or even no preliminary sketches but embarked immediately on the final work, while others prepared their pictures with many sketches and detailed studies.

The normal though by no means universal progression begins with the composition sketches, moves on to studies in perspective and proportion which serve to clarify the general design of the picture, and culminates in studies of

JEAN-AUGUSTE-DOMINIQUE INGRES (Montauban 1780–1867 Paris) *Lute player*. Pencil. British Museum, London. Study for the picture *Odalisque à l'Esclave* in Baltimore. Ingres' pencil drawings, which are usually very delicate, are characterized by clear and unbroken lines. The classical heroism and pathos of his teacher David *(Ill. 16)* are reflected in milder form in Ingres' intimate treatment of his subjects

movement, drawings of drapery and detail, which finally determine the form and content of the picture, often down to the smallest detail. There is one sheet extant, which is exceptionally rare for the fifteenth century. It contains all three phases of a preparatory sketch for a monumental composition on both sides of the paper. These are the rough drawings for a *Vision of St Francis* by Ghirlandaio now in the Gabinetto Nazionale delle Stampe in Rome. The first is a rapid sketch of the wall on which the picture is to be painted, showing the architectonic setting. Then follows a more detailed sketch of the proposed composition, with the perspective of the room in which the scene is to be set precisely traced in *(Ill. 13)*. For many of these Renaissance drawings, tracing was almost a mathematical exercise. The positions to be taken up by the main figures are already indicated. These preparatory and composition sketches are followed by a more complete drawing with more detailed indications of where and how the figures will appear *(Ill. 14)*.

Until the form and content of the picture were finally decided, changes could always be made. A page from a Veronese sketchbook in the Albertina, with composition and figure studies for a historical painting in the Palace of the Doges, shows how the artist experimented with various possibilities. In searching for the appropriate composition, the artist enables us to follow closely the growth of the creative process *(Ill. 12)*. A fine example of a complete composition with particular emphasis on the architectonic arrangement of the figures – also showing each single figure as a geometric form – is a drawing by Luca Cambiaso for a Resurrection *(Ill. 15)*.

The final stage of the composition sketches comes with the rough drawing, in which the picture is already nearing completion and which may even incorporate the results of the detail studies. These drawings served as a basis for the finished work. They might be passed on to other artists; this was the usual practice in the case of drawings for the applied arts or painting on glass. But pictures were also painted from such drawings both in the draughtsman's workshop and by other artists. Vasari reports, for example, that Simone Martini prepared a drawing for an altarpiece at Pistoia which Lippo Memmi painted. Michelangelo gave such drawings away, and Dürer, Guilio Romano, Rubens and many others passed rough drawings on to others for them to complete the pictures.

III RAFFAELLO SANTI known as RAPHAEL (Urbino 1483–1520 Rome)
Study sheet. Pen with bistre and red chalk, *c.* 1507. 256:184 mm. Albertina, Vienna. Cat. III, 53 verso. Fischl (1922) 111.
From Raphael's Florentine sketchbook, in which variants on the theme 'Virgin and Child' are tried out. The figure top right was used in the *Madonna Colonna*, the position of the figure left centre occurs again in the *Madonna Niccolini*. On the front side of the sheet a preliminary drawing for the Madonna in Bridgewater House (*c.* 1507)

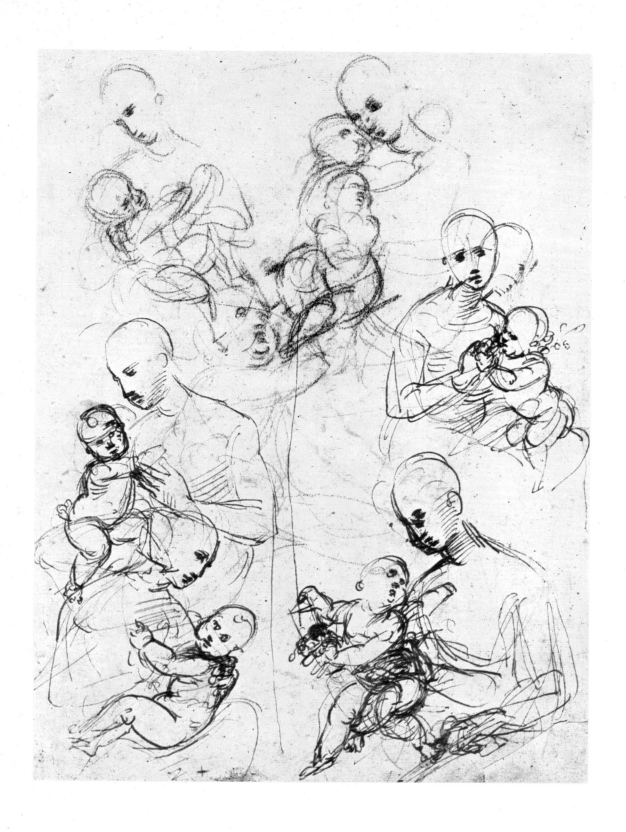

Rough drawings may exhibit certain distinct characteristics, depending upon their function. However, these naturally do not follow any hard and fast rules.

A visible sign of preparatory drawings for large-scale works is the screen, an orthogonal, usually square, network of lines which is drawn over the picture, dividing the composition into sections which can then be transposed more easily to the larger screen on the final picture *(cf. Ill. 16)*. If the screen appears under the drawing, this means a transfer was made from a model or the drawing was done with the help of an optical device, as in Dürer's woodcut of the screen draughtsman (Ill. p. 141). This transfer method was usually employed for studies of perspective. But most drawings on a screen are for the purpose of enlarging on the rough drawing. When this type of drawing is full-size and ready to be directly transposed on to the wall, canvas or panel, it is known as a 'cartoon'. This corresponds to the working drawing for architecture, glass-painting or the (always reversed) drawing for tapestries. As these cartoons had a direct, practical application and were indeed frequently prepared by apprentices, few of the earlier specimens have survived and those that have are seldom intact. We know what became of Leonardo da Vinci's and Michelangelo's cartoons for the frescoes in the Sala della Signoria in the Palazzo Vecchio in Florence which never materialized. They were exhibited for so long and copied so often as famous compositions that they finally fell to pieces. The custom of drawing cartoons completely replaced the medieval wall drawing, particularly in Italy. These cartoons, most of them purely linear and devoid of artistic ambition, were either impressed with a stylus–the back of the paper could be coloured in order to bring out the impression–or, much more frequently, the drawing was punctured with holes along the contour lines. Charcoal or ochre dust was then 'pounced' through the holes to indicate the principal lines and so provide points of reference for the painter. Traces of these impressed or punctured lines can still be seen on many frescoes *(cf. Ill. 18)*. Impressing or puncturing was also employed for copying purposes, and many a picture–the Holbein portraits at Windsor for example–bear the marks of this crude process.

As cartoons were designed to serve a specific practical purpose, colour was rarely introduced and as a rule no attempt was even made to give depth to the

Albrecht Dürer (Nuremberg 1471–1528)
The Visitation. Pen in grey, *c.* 1504. 225:207 mm. Albertina, Vienna. Winkler 293.
Preliminary drawing for a woodcut of the life of the Virgin. Clear pen drawing, large format, without cross-hatching or small curves. The monogram appears in reverse for printing. The small dog appears to have been modelled on the dog in *Madonna with the many animals* (Plate IV)

lines. Only in the cartoons for Gobelin tapestries were colours used, since here it was essential to the basic pattern. Raphael's sketches for the tapestries in the Sistine Chapel, now in the Victoria and Albert Museum in London, were done in watercolours. A pre-painting treatment was also given to drawings for glass paintings, mostly small in size, which were popular at the beginning of the sixteenth century, especially in Switzerland and north Germany but also in the Netherlands. In contrast to the medieval working drawings for coloured glass, wash drawings could also be employed for the new painting technique. Many of the drawings for later glass paintings were only identifiable as such by superficial features like format or basic composition (cf. Ill. 41).

A fairly safe way to recognize a drawing intended for engraving is the fact that the picture is reversed. If the composition runs from right to left, if individual figures are seen to be acting in reverse, such as holding a weapon in the left hand, or if inscriptions, monograms and figures appear as if reflected in a mirror, then one can safely assume that this is a drawing for an engraving. But one must also bear in mind that the originality of the artist could be seriously inhibited, if, as was frequently the case, he was making a practice copy of a reproduction engraving which was already reversed. The engraver's working drawings also reproduce the model in reverse. It is often only possible to distinguish between the original drawing and the copy, if one is familiar with the style of the original draughtsman. And finally a drawing can also be reproduced in reverse by the transfer technique: the original is moistened and placed under pressure on a sheet of absorbent paper. The picture now appears as in a mirror, but thin and smooth and flat-surfaced. Transfers were also made in order to supply a large number of copies.

Sketches for woodcuts are characterized by simple, clear lines, which are unbroken and avoid tight curves (cf. Ill. p. 37). Other characteristics are parallel hatches fairly widely spaced, and uncoordinated white and black areas. Yet the sixteenth century also produced woodcuts based on drawings with cross-hatches and minute details. So refined had the technique of the woodcut become, in fact, that it could reproduce almost all the subtleties of a pen-and-ink drawing, so that the preparatory sketch needed to take virtually no account of technical considerations. In many cases the final drawing had been transferred direct to the wood block and,

IV ALBRECHT DÜRER (Nuremberg 1471–1528)
Madonna with the many animals. Pen and ink, watercolour, *c.* 1503. 321:243 mm. Albertina, Vienna. Cat. IV., 50. Winkler 296.
Complete harmony of thin lines and delicate colours, producing a self-contained composition which Dürer returned to again and again (first version in Berlin, another in the Louvre). A network of squares just visible over Mary and the fox suggests that the artist intended to enlarge this drawing

like drawings made direct on a wall or panel, become completely identified with the end-product. A few of these wood blocks with preliminary drawings have been preserved in cases where the composition was rejected or unfinished.

A drawing for a copper-engraving requires a sharp burin and a pen, which can cope with the hard material. Features of this particular medium are clear contours with smooth-flowing lines, cross-hatches and also stippling, but not flat half-tones or large areas of black. In the case of works by artists who are *peintres-graveurs*, that is both draughtsmen and engravers, the formal relationship between independent drawing and preparatory drawing is so close that it is virtually impossible to distinguish one from the other. A drawing 'in the engraving style' such as the *Head of Mercury* by Hendrik Goltzius shows how profoundly conscious the artist was, in making this pen-and-ink drawing, of the technical requirements of engraving (Ill. p. 39). The skilfully developed technique of mezzotint reproductions in the seventeenth century also gave much greater scope to drawings for copper-engravings and still more for etchings. Van Dyck, for example, in making his sketches for his *Iconography*, a collection of portraits of outstanding artists, was comparatively unhindered by technical considerations *(Ill. 5)*.

Printmaking processes also affected methods of drawing, one example being the stipple method of the Flemish artists Jan Wierx and Crispin de Passe. The mutual effect on each other of printmaking methods and styles of drawing continued until well into the eighteenth century. Thus in the drawings of the illustrator Charles Eisen there are distinct graphic elements, and Daniel Chodowiecki's frequent practice of scratching out the highlights was derived from the old mezzotints.

The specific features of a preparatory drawing for a particular graphic reproductive process began to disappear as the highly specialized engravers overcame the material problems.

Drawings for goldsmiths' work and applied arts require particularly clear contours and a sharp definition of the different planes. Here a somewhat dry style of draughtsmanship is usually a feature of the working drawing, which eventually brings out certain areas in terms both of plane and of colour. Frequently, where a drawing is symmetrical, only one half is completed, the other being merely roughed in or transferred by printing or tracing.

HENDRIK GOLTZIUS (Mühlbrecht near Venlo 1558–1617 Haarlem) ▶
Head of Mercury. Pen and dark brown ink, 1587. 450:366 mm. Ashmolean Museum, Oxford. Reznicek 119.
Goltzius specialized in engraving from foreign models. In this, his own drawing, he set out to employ the method of copper-engraving, achieving plastic values by means of lines that swell and fade in very precise parallel groupings

HGoltzius. fecit. A°.1587.

10 ANTONIO PISANELLO

(Pisa 1395–before 1455 Verona (?))

Study sheet. Pen in brown on parchment, 165:220 mm. Boymans–van Beuningen Museum, Rotterdam. Reproduction in original size.

The juxtaposition of a religious scene and studies in the nude in one drawing reflects the transition from the medieval to the Renaissance studio. The traditional Annunciation scene is drawn with simple, unbroken lines which are highly ornamental. The 'more modern' nude studies employ hatched modelling in order to bring out bodies and movement. Model drawing and life study, like the battle scene on the other side, served as a pattern for further work.

11 MICHAEL WOLGEMUT (Nuremberg 1434–1519)

Pattern sheet. Pen in brown on red-tinted paper, 294:201 mm. Staatliche Graphische Sammlung, Munich.

This collection of various head-dresses is an *aide-mémoire*, put together from various sketches and used for several works. In utilitarian drawings of this kind the artist's personal style is naturally more difficult to recognize.

12 PAOLO CALIARI, known as VERONESE

(Verona 1528–88 Venice)

Sketch sheet. Pen in bistre with wash, 298:217 mm. Albertina, Vienna. Cat. I, 108; Tietze 2152.

This is part of one of Veronese's sketchbooks and shows different rough drawings for two historical pictures in the Palace of the Doges, which were only completed after Veronese's death. The repeated inscription 'Capitanino' in the artist's own hand refers to the Doge, who is welcoming the pope to Venice (above: 'Capitanino gradiscente il Papa a Venezia'). Below right: the collector's mark of Luigi Grassi (Lugt 1171b).

13 DOMENICO GHIRLANDAIO (Florence 1449–94)

Apparition of St Francis. Pen in brown. Detail from the back of *Ill. 14*.

14 DOMENICO GHIRLANDAIO (Florence 1449–94)

Apparition of St Francis. Pen in brown, light wash, 198:218 mm. Gabinetto Nazionale delle Stampe, Rome. Berenson 890.

Two stages in the artistic creation of a large composition, presumably for a mural. After a systematic construction sketch came a drawing in which the figures were positioned *(Ill. 13)* and then a further, more complete drawing *(Ill. 14)*. The next stages were presumably a fully detailed drawing and a full-size cartoon.

15 LUCA CAMBIASO

(Moneglia/Genoa 1527–85 Escorial)

Resurrection and Ascension. Pen in brown, wash, 320:228 mm. Gabinetto Nazionale delle Stampe, Rome.

In order to give his drawings for large-scale murals an impression of monumental size and at the same time to control the architectonic cohesion of his compositions, Luca Cambiaso adopted an abstract style of drawing. The reduction of the figures to geometrical terms resembles in many points of detail the cubist drawings of the twentieth century. Attempts had already been made before Cambiaso's time to discover geometrical rules governing the human body (Dürer, Schön); after his time his method of clarifying problems of composition was widely followed in drawings for monumental paintings.

16 JACQUES-LOUIS DAVID (Paris 1784–1825 Brussels)

Study of a seated woman. Black chalk, white relief, 1783. 505:350 mm. Musée Bonnat, Bayonne.

This drawing of a woman in the classical pose of sorrow has been squared for transfer to a picture. While in the drawing, apart from its statuesque calm and clarity of line, there are traces of the dainty refinement of the rococo in the details, the finished painting in the Louvre is wholly classical.

17 PIETER VAN DER FAES (PETER LELY)

(Soest near Utrecht 1618–80 London)

Standard-bearer. Black charcoal, white relief, on blue-grey paper, 500:234 mm. British Museum, London. Cat. B. D. Lely 1.

This is one of a series of drawings showing participants in the procession of the Order of the Garter. In view of the subject, the artist is naturally interested in detail, but this does not preclude broad, painterly lines with oiled charcoal, which gives a particularly deep, soft line, although it often impregnates the paper and leaves greasy edges along the lines.

18 ANDREA VERROCCHIO (Florence 1436–88 Venice)

Head of an Angel. Pen and charcoal over a pencil sketch, 210:180 mm. Florence, Uffizi. Berenson 2781. Reproduction in original size.

Fragment of an original cartoon. The main contours show traces of a regular series of holes; and the marks of the transfer with charcoal dust are still visible in places.

10

8461

12

13

14

15

16

17

18

Most of these pictorially complete drawings were preceded by studies and sketches of individual figures, groups of figures, important objects and details. Here, drawing for purposes of practice becomes almost indistinguishable from the deliberate study. When the artist is treating the sort of conventional theme that frequently recurs, he can fall back on previous drawings he has made or employ accepted models by other masters. Borrowing in this way was frequently practised from one generation to another and was not regarded as plagiarism. The concept of a personal copyright in artistic creation developed late, and absolute originality is quite a modern requirement. This explains how so many details – figures in conventional postures and even landscapes, architectural scenes and objects of all kinds – constantly reappear within an artistic circle that is often quite extensive. Studies for animal drawings in particular, which sometimes required models that were hard to come by, were frequently used in this way. In Dürer's pen and water-colour picture of the *Madonna with the many animals* (Plate IV) the owl, the dog (Ill. p. 39), the goldfinch and the parrot can also be seen in other works of his.

Drawings on recurrent themes were also used for pictures produced at very different periods of time. In many cases only a minor alteration is needed, such as a slight change in the attitude of a head, in order to form the nucleus of a new composition. Raphael's studies for a *Madonna and Child* (Plate III) provided a stimulus for several pictures.

Drawings, engravings, pictures and even sculptures were to some extent among the 'studio props', which included not merely objects of daily use but also interesting, exotic objects, materials and costumes, weapons and an infinite variety of things that were used as accessories. Drawings of such objects must have been prepared in large numbers; and indeed whole collections may have been put together; one example showing various types of head-dress has been preserved from the Wolgemut workshop and shows how the medieval practice of using pattern-books continued in this form *(Ill. 11)*.

Where the artist was unable to find a suitable formula in the collection of pattern drawings or from his own experience, he had to use actual models in the appropriate pose. Drawings of apprentices in conventional poses as well as illustrations of studios at work show who was called upon to act as model. The realization that an organically accurate figure could only be portrayed if the artist had a detailed knowledge of human anatomy led to life-studies and also to what was in effect a medical examination of the skeleton and the muscles. The 'Academy' at the court of the Medici in Florence openly acknowledged the close relationship between science and art. Its most distinguished exponent was Leonardo da Vinci. Since then drawing from life has remained standard practice in the training of a painter; many compositions have begun as life studies. Members of the studio again acted as models, but professional models were occasionally used too. For female figures, however, young male apprentices often had to be used or previous works, usually from antiquity, were taken as models. The comparative freedom of the bathing establishments, from which Pisanello *(cf. Ill. 10)* and more especially the Dutch and German painters obtained their models, disappeared in the Reformation and Counter-Reformation periods. In the official academies not even a clothed female model was admissible until the eighteenth century.

The postures of the figures for a particular composition, especially in the mannerist period, were often so complicated and so awkward for the models that artificial aids had to be used. These can occasionally be spotted in the drawings and sometimes they were even included as a part of them. A stick was often used to help the model keep his balance or prevent an upraised arm from tiring. Tintoretto's sketches frequently show figures on ropes *(Ill. 22)*. A sling was employed to immobilize individual limbs in outstretched positions. Suspended or falling postures were usually drawn from a reclining model and then adjusted to bring them into the desired position.

A fairly common substitute for the live model was the marionette *(manicchino)* or the small clay or wax figure which could be set or hung up in the desired position. Such models were used both for anatomical study and, dressed in pieces of material or glued paper, to study drapery.

Studies of clothing and highly detailed drawings of materials and their peculiarities in folds and free fall form a major and essential part of these study drawings.

Particularly important and difficult details called for intensive work, which explains why drawings of heads and hands, often on the same sheet, constantly recur *(cf. Ill. 49)*. Many famous examples, such as Dürer's *Hands in Prayer*, began as studies of this kind. Of particular interest are the changes made in the process of the work. An entire composition can be radically transformed by just a few lines drawn over the first rough sketch *(cf. Plates III, V)*. The original contours which have been either left or only slightly masked are direct evidence of the genesis of the artistic process. These *pentimenti*, or 'repentances', as they are

V LEONARDO DA VINCI (Vinci 1452–1519 Amboise)
Study of drapery. Silverpoint, brush in white, white relief, black shading on red tinted paper. 256:195 mm. Gabinetto Nazionale delle Stampe, Rome. Popham 1.
The various stages of the work are clearly apparent: preliminary drawing and corrections with silverpoint to head and upper part of body; application of Chinese white with point of brush; and plastic modelling by means of dark shadows in the drapery of the kneeling figure, which was doubtless designed to be the figure of the Madonna in an Annunciation

not very logically called, frequently occur in isolated studies and reflect the constant search for the definitive form. A partial alteration could also be achieved by covering over the rejected part and drawing afresh. Not infrequently those parts which were usually painted over with white have become visible again, thus revealing two or more versions simultaneously. Another method of correction was to gum over parts of the drawing. This process can also be employed as a simple form of alternative sketch, where the superimposed part is only attached on one side and can therefore be turned over.

To erase or wipe out an entire drawing is only possible by certain technical methods. Soft pencil or chalk was removed with breadcrumbs before rubber was used. But it was more usual, particularly in sketches, either to juxtapose or to superimpose the various experiments, and this is in fact a further indication of their practical purpose.

Nature Studies

Interest in a realistic portrayal of every detail is particularly marked north of the Alps, and many drawings may have been motivated by a sort of graphic curiosity rather than by any more specific objective. Nature studies can give the impression of having been drawn as an end in themselves, of being formally complete. There are many examples of this in Dürer's work. But marginal notes on colour or other details are a clear indication that the drawings in question were deliberately designed for more ambitious works. That special importance was attached to them as authentic nature studies can be inferred from the fact that the phrase 'from life' is frequently written on them. 'Naert leven' appears on a whole group of Bruegel drawings *(cf. Ill. 2)*. There is, then, an almost imperceptible transition to drawings which are not essentially utilitarian showing episodes from everyday life, characteristic types, animals and plants, and finally landscapes.

The term 'nature study' covers two quite distinct categories of drawing. Studies 'from nature' were always part of an artist's training. They were in preparation for a larger composition or done simply as a form of practice current ever since the first drawing was made. Studies 'in nature', which are characteristic

VI Hans Holbein the Younger (Augsburg 1497–1543 London) ►
Portrait of Dorothea Meyer, née Kannengiesser. Black and coloured chalks on paper grounded with Chinese white, 1525/26. 394:281 mm. Kupferstichkabinett, Basle. Ganz 15.
This study of a kneeling nun for the Darmstadt Madonna is so nearly complete that it might rank as an independent portrait. In the painting, the cloth covering the head and chin is not shown. The soft chalks and firm yet relaxed line produce a very lifelike picture

features of certain comparatively limited periods, are quite different. Strictly speaking, of course, all model studies are 'from nature', whether the models involved are figures or specific parts of the body, movements or draperies, animals, plants or any other objects. Nature studies, as successors to the pattern-books and frequently performing the same functions, began to play an increasingly important role from the early Renaissance onwards. Pure practice drawings and nature studies with a practical purpose in mind are joined by drawings which, though without any utilitarian motive, cannot yet be regarded as independent works of art in themselves. They are designed to some extent as additions to the artist's repertoire. Early examples are Jacopo Bellini's sketch books in London and Paris, and among the best known examples are Dürer's animal and plant studies. His watercolours in particular are remarkable for the passionate interest they show in nature, representing a break with a centuries-old tradition. The illustrated medical books (*Herbarium* of Dioscorides) were part of a tradition of plant drawing which dated back to antiquity and which usually clung to the style of later antiquity. But Dürer had apparently dug out a piece of turf, carried it off to study and drawn it from various angles and in various forms. These drawings reflect the same scientific curiosity, the same highly significant phenomenon of humanism that we find in its purest and most coherent expression in Leonardo's studies and writings.

Although it is implicit in a nature study that the appearance of an object should be portrayed as objectively as possible, no reproduction, however faithful, could fail to be influenced by contemporary style and environment. Characteristic of fifteenth- and sixteenth-century nature studies, particularly north of the Alps, is precise reproduction, rich in detail, executed with scrupulous care and with a marked emphasis on spatial and physical portrayal. This descriptive naturalism remains a feature of Dutch art throughout the entire seventeenth century. The draughtsmen of the early nineteenth century quite consciously and systematically adopted both the technique and the mental approach of the early nature studies. This impersonal, to some extent tradesmanlike, neat style of drawing pursues its own special course through the whole of the nineteenth century and has reappeared in the present time with the artists of the 'new realism' school and in part also with the Surrealists and their successors.

The interest in the object, which naturally varies with the period, is also conditioned by the temperament of the artist himself. Highly individual styles, such as mannerism – which in drawing is one of the most productive and varied – or the modern trends reveal a conscious preoccupation with form in the nature studies. The *Bagful of Nuts*, in which Tintoretto highlighted the muscular formation of his models, is an example of the frankly descriptive style of drawing which is to be found above all in drawings by strong artistic personalities, sometimes

JOSEPH ANTON KOCH (Obergibeln, Tyrol 1768–1839 Rome)
Study of leaves, Pencil, 125:165 mm. Kupferstichkabinett, Akademie der bildenden Künste, Vienna. Lutterotti 910–922. Detail from a page of a sketchbook.
For the German neoclassicists, drawing from nature was an essential prerequisite for their landscapes and compositions, which, though based on classical principles, had many romantic features

bearing their own signature but always with something in common. Rembrandt's animal studies as well as the drawings by Rubens and his closest associates are worth mentioning in this context.

The French painters of the eighteenth century, in particular, such as Watteau (Plate XV), Fragonard, Boucher, Lancret *(Ill. 25)*, and Venetians such as Tiepolo *(Ill. 47)* and Piazzetta *(Ill. 49)* interpreted the natural models in their studies according to their own artistic style. The studies of the classical, Nazarene and romantic masters – David, Ingres, Overbeck, Schnorr von Carolsfeld – who were much more austere, more matter-of-fact and more interested in plastic values, were followed by a freer interpretation of the natural model, a 'notation of the optical impression', as in Delacroix and Géricault. Both conceptions ran side by side throughout the nineteenth century with only minor variations of time and place. While the mannered drawing of the academies continued until well into the twentieth century to cling to the objective reproduction of the natural model, the leading forward-looking artists, starting with the impressionists, adopted a subjective approach to the object as their guiding rule. And all the formal principles of the various schools are reflected in their graphic studies. In the drawings of the impressionists and post-impressionists the object is presented as seen through the eye of the artist. Menzel's studies, for instance, as the written inscriptions also make clear, are more concerned with atmospheric effects of light than with the physical composition of the object *(Ill. 8)*. Klimt's lines have an ornamental quality which in no way detracts from the vibrant dynamism of the surface

(Ill. 9), whereas in Picasso or Matisse *(Ill. 55)*, for example, the construction of the picture has again become more marked, even in the studies.

Landscape Drawings

Drawing in nature, in other words landscape drawing, was dominated for a long time by interest in a particular motif. Landscape drawings, like paintings, were a collection of individual experiences drawn together into an imaginary world landscape. Actual views such as the drawings and watercolours of Leonardo and Dürer can hardly have been the first nature studies (many of the landscapes in Jacopo Bellini's sketchbooks would probably rank as such). The Alpine landscape reappears in drawings of the Danube school *(cf. Ill. 40)* – Wolf Huber is known to have drawn 'landscape portraits' – and among the Dutch. Ever since the sixteenth century, the latter had been travelling more and more frequently to Rome, the place with the greatest concentration of antique art; their sketchbooks are filled with views of the Eternal City which are also topographically accurate.

With the beginning of the seventeenth century, drawing 'in nature' began to take on a special importance in Rome. The work of the Dutch artists in particular was given written recognition by Sandrart and there is also pictorial documentation, such as Jan Asselijn's drawing, now in Berlin, in which he portrayed a group of his colleagues working in the open air *(Ill. 3)*. For the most part, however, these nature studies merely prepared the ground for subsequent expansion. Thus the drawings of such important landscape painters as Adam Elsheimer, Paul Bril, Annibale Carracci and Domenichino, were already 'composed' with the final painting in mind and sometimes even formed a section of it; the structure of the final picture predetermines the drawing. Carracci builds up his *Landscape with Bridge* in stratified, almost parallel layers with expressive overtones *(Ill. 42)*. The atmosphere of Claude Lorrain's idealized Campagna landscape, in which the sloping hills gradually lead the eye into the distance, seems discreet by comparison *(Ill. 43)*.

From the sixteenth century onwards the *vedute*, which aimed at topographical precision, often with the help of optical instruments, formed a special branch of landscape drawing. But the dominant interest was always in 'picturesque' motifs, such as the broken-down gateway in Salvator Rosa's masterly brush drawing *(Ill. 6)*. The baroque landscape is composed of just such nature studies, which almost have the appearance of stage-settings. By employing *repoussoir* motifs – disproportionately large objects such as clumps of bushes or trees, undulations in the ground or even figures in the foreground – the impression of depth is heightened. Similarly roads, rivers and mountain-chains, which lead the eye into the distant

VII WILLIAM TURNER (London 1775–1851 Chelsea). *View of Venice from the Lagoon.*
Pen, chalk and watercolour over a pencil sketch, *c.* 1835. 222:295 mm. Fitzwilliam Museum,
Cambridge.
Turner used watercolour to turn the various objects, outlined with soft pencil strokes, into a
romantic vision of light and colour. Works of this kind are on the limits of 'drawing'

combines great fidelity, which in some of the drawings can only have been achieved with the help of optical instruments, with a tenderness of colouring that makes his portraits seem alive. In these studies, drawn directly from the model with a clear gradation of priorities, one can trace every stage of the drawing process, from the incredibly finely-drawn features of the face to the superficial strokes of the drapery. The drawings leave a more vivid impression than the completed pictures (Plate VI). Holbein's approach to portraiture and his style of drawing were adopted by François Clouet in France. Portrait drawing like portrait painting became more and more specialized. In the sixteenth and especially the seventeeth centuries, on the other hand, its status as a relatively independent form of art was considerably reduced and the drawing was again considered mainly as a preparation for the painted portait and subordinated to it. In the course of the sixteenth century the sometimes almost prosaic portrayal of the sitter's outward appearance, which one finds in the Renaissance portraits, is heavily overlaid by the contemporary ideal. Michelangelo's heads, most of which are drawn with red chalk, are characteristically solemn and austere. They stand by themselves quite independently of the portrait as such, even when a specific model is known to have been used (Plate X).

The character heads, which began with Leonardo's studies and became increasingly popular, are also a departure from the conventional portrait; they mark the beginning of caricature with its exaggeration and distortion. While this type of portrait retained the linear character of a drawing, studies for portraits were increasingly influenced by the principles of painting; in their preference for softer materials and for multicoloured chalks and in their use of the brush. Yet the drawings still remain closer to the model, are 'more faithful' than the completed painted portraits. Rubens' drawing for the portrait of Isabella Brant shows clearly how the artist progressed step by step from the pencil drawing to the use of white relief and colour tones (Plate VIII). Van Dyck, moreover, also used this drawing as a basis for a portrait. Unlike other portrait painters such as Velazquez, who have left no preliminary sketches, Van Dyck not only made drawings in preparation for his portraits, he also made drawings for prints, a technique closer to that of drawing. But here too he introduced certain essential elements of painting such as washes, soft chalks and heightened effects of light *(Ill. 5)*.

VIII PETER PAUL RUBENS (Siegen 1577–1640 Antwerp)
Portrait of Isabella Brant. Black and red chalk, heightened with white, reinforced with pen and brush, 381:292 mm. British Museum, London. Burchard–d'Hulst 135.
Drawing for the portrait of 1626 in the Uffizi. Life study with considerable painterly detail such as use of ink to underline the irises and eyelashes and use of brush for the nostrils. Below right: collectors' marks (P. H. Lankrink, L. 2090; J. Richardson Sr, L. 2184; Earl Spencer, L. 1532)

The interest in physiognomy, which is such a marked feature of Rembrandt's drawings and which, despite Raphael's rather sober, 'objective' treatment in his portrait of Castiglione, nevertheless turns a quick sketch into a human study, was subordinated in the later seventeenth and particularly in the eighteenth centuries to the desire to make portraits representative. These official portrait drawings, which frequently began as sketches for engravings and are surrounded by all kinds of decorative emblems, are in sharp contrast to the more intimate studies, in many of which the portrait is built into an appropriate setting. Fragonard, for example, portrayed his sister-in-law Marguerite Gérard drawing a religious composition *(Ill. 27)*, and the friendship portraits of the romantics and Nazarenes were drawn while they were working in the open air *(cf. Ill. 4)*. This pictorial extension of the portrait again gave it a passing resemblance to the independent drawing. The frontiers between study, sketch and final work disappeared altogether with the pastel portraits of the eighteenth century *(cf.* Plate XI). Following the idealistic conception of portraiture in baroque and classical times came another naturalistic period in the early nineteenth century, when the accepted style was one of minute observation and the figuration of the face was 'modelled' by means of groups of concurrent strokes. In modern portrait drawings which, in keeping with the general tendency to rate the drawing as a work of art, are for the most part recognized as independent works, problems of form and a profound interest in psychology become increasingly important. The early portraits of Oskar Kokoschka are particularly striking examples of this dual function of portrait drawing *(cf.* the portrait of Herwarth Walden, editor of the periodical *Sturm*; Ill. p. 67). The expressive qualities, both the spiritual and intellectual personality of the subject and the artist's expression of him, take priority over the immediate resemblance. This is particularly apparent in the self-portraits. The relatively large number of self-portraits is due not merely to the fact that the model is always available but also to the greater freedom the artist enjoys *vis-à-vis* his 'employer'. Self-portraits are not dependent on the personal wishes of a patron. They are motivated much more by the artistic act itself than by interest in a 'finished' work and are therefore often sketches. The human and artistic development of artists such as Dürer, Rembrandt, Van Gogh, Max Beckmann and Egon Schiele, who drew many self-portraits, can be followed very closely and clearly.

A special form of portraiture, which deliberately exploits the graphic properties of drawing, is caricature. One of its characteristic features is the expressive exaggeration of realistic details, a reduction to certain formulas, which themselves can become meaningful. The artistic caricature, which begins with the Carraccis, is distinct from the character studies which Leonardo made popular and the various comic drawings. Bernini is known to have made caricatures of certain personalities

(Scipione Borghese). Portrait caricature again became prominent in the nineteenth century with the works of Goya, Isabey *(Ill. 50)*, Daumier and Toulouse-Lautrec; and in the twentieth century it was followed by the political caricature.

OSKAR KOKOSCHKA (Pöchlarn 1886)
Portrait of Herwarth Walden. Brush and pen in black ink, 1910. 285:222 mm. Fogg Art Museum, Harvard University, Cambridge, Mass.
Kokoschka's portraits are less concerned with a naturalistic likeness than with a psychological projection of the personality. By means of formal exaggeration, which sometimes borders on the ornamental, he achieves a portrayal of the subject which is also graphically expressive

67

19 PIETRO PERUGINO
(Castel della Pieve 1450–1523 Fortignano)
Sibyl. Pen in bistre over pencil sketch, 1509. 304:84 mm. Uffizi, Florence.
Drawing for the fresco in the Audience Chamber of the 'Cambio' in Perugia. Plastic and pictorial elements are expressed by linear graphic means such as heavy contours and parallel hatching.

20 FRANCESCO GIROLAMO MAZZOLA, known as PARMIGIANINO (Parma 1503–40 Casal Maggiore)
Circe and Odysseus' comrades. Brush in bistre over black chalk, wash, heightened with white, on brown tinted paper, 219:206 mm. Uffizi, Florence. Copertini 979. Slightly reduced detail.
Pronounced painterly contrasts of light and shade have been applied over the drawing with a soft, wet brush, but without affecting the character of the lines.

21 GIORGIO VASARI (Arezzo 1511–74 Florence)
Figure in back view. Detail from *The Capture of Vico Pisano*. Brush and pen in dark brown, heightened with white, 378:180 mm. Uffizi, Florence.
The plastic modelling of the central figure is achieved with a dry, pointed brush and pen following graphic, linear principles. By reversing the customary pattern of chiaroscuro, the stylized effect is further heightened.

22 JACOPO ROBUSTI, known as TINTORETTO
(Venice 1518–94)
Male nude. Charcoal, 328:227 mm. Albertina, Vienna. Cat. I. 90; Tietze 1752.
Study from a model who is holding on to a rope. The short, tightly-curved strokes give the exaggerated muscles an optical-painterly rather than a tactile-plastic quality.

23 BARTHOLOMÄUS SPRANGER
(Antwerp 1546–1611 Prague)
Apollo. Pen in olive brown on paper lightly grounded with black chalk, 203:140 mm. Albertina, Vienna. Cat. II. 283.
Characteristic of the leading master of the mannerist artists at the court of Rudolf II in Prague is the contradiction between the boldness of the design and the nervous bittiness of the drawing.

24 JACOPO CARRUCCI known as PONTORMO
(Pontormo 1494–1557 Florence)
Rider. Black chalk, 1522–25. 403:270 mm. Uffizi, Florence. Berenson 2250; Rearich 230.
Bold ,'open' style of drawing producing monumental effect. Study for the fresco *Passage of the Israelites through the desert* for the Certosa in Pavia.

25 NICOLAS LANCRET (Paris 1690–1754)
Study sheet. Red ochre, white and black chalk on grey natural paper, 265:299 mm. Louvre, Paris. Cat. gen. 5637.
The use of varicoloured chalks on tinted paper is in keeping with the basic approach of eighteenth-century painters. The lines are relaxed, often blurred. The arrangement of the individual studies on the one sheet of paper also shows his preference for a lively and decorative design.

26 JACQUES CALLOT (?) (Nancy 1592–1635)
Sketch sheet. Pen and ink, 117:90 mm. Louvre, Paris. Cat. gen. 25058. Detail in original size.
The drawings of Callot and his imitators have a casual air with details simply and briefly notated. The picturesque style of these drawings is the graphic equivalent of the artist's favourite subjects: soldiers, beggars, figures from Italian comedy and popular types.

27 JEAN-HONORÉ FRAGONARD
(Grasse 1732–1806 Paris)
Woman drawing. Brush in bistre over lead pencil drawing, 451:338 mm. Albertina, Vienna.
Fragonard's sister-in-law, Marguerite Gérard, was the model for this drawing, which combines a genre-type study with a well-calibrated composition, almost classical in its severity, of interwoven triangles. With its contrasting effects of light and deep shadow, this brush drawing has the attributes of an independent work.

28 GIOVANNI BATTISTA PIRANESI
(Mogliano 1720–78 Rome)
Roman prison. Pen and ink wash over pencil drawing, 256:189 mm. Kunsthalle, Hamburg. Thomas 7. Reproduction in original size.
Piranesi's fantastic architectural effects were inspired by the ancient ruins of Rome and even in this small format the exaggerated perspective and dramatic shadows produce an effect of oppressive monumentality.

29 LEONARDO DA VINCI (Vinci 1452–1519 Amboise)
Proemio (Rain). Black chalk, pen with brown and yellowish-brown ink; after 1512. 162:203 mm. Royal Library, Windsor Castle. Berenson 12445; Popham 296. Reproduction in original size.
This drawing is one of a series of studies in which Leonardo set out to record the atmospheric conditions which lead to a storm. Various inks are used to highlight the individual currents. Example of a scientific drawing with great artistic merit.

19

20

21

22

23

24

25

26

27

28

29

Illustration Drawings

Illustration drawings represent the final stage in the artistic drawing process. Yet they are not independent in the sense of being entirely self-contained works. They are tied to a text, in other words subject to an order which lies outside the world of pictorial art, and frequently they are also tied in the sense that they are preliminary drawings for some multiple reproduction process. Both these ties can be very close; on the other hand they can be so loose as to permit a large measure of independence. Book illustration in the printed book fulfils the same decorative and didactic function that was previously performed by the illumination of manuscripts. And from illumination it has also inherited the two essential types of illustration: the full-page illustration and the graphic contribution to the printed page which illustrates the text. The full-page illustration comes very close to being a self-contained work. Often covering the entire page, but usually surrounded by a margin which also gives it the outward appearance of a separate composition, it is either situated opposite the text on a page by itself or at least occupies an equivalent space. It is always clearly separated from the text.

Where picture and text share the same page, the object is always to combine them into one decorative whole.

As in illumination, so too in illustration the initial letter, the first capital in a chapter or verse, is a vehicle for bringing picture and script together in richly ornamented form. Moreover margins are often filled with delicate floral or abstract decoration, which also spills over into the printed lines. Frequently this ornamentation is enlivened with allegorical and even grotesque designs (drolleries). A formal stress on the margin is achieved by the framelike border, which, so to speak, brackets the text.

In this type of illustration, the decorative unity of text and picture and the superficial character of the page are particularly clearly preserved. But the link becomes more tenuous the more the illustrated book resembles a picture-book. A shift in the relationship between picture and text produces a continuous pictorial narrative with an accompanying text, which now explains the pictures to a greater extent than the pictures illustrated the text. The series of pictures becomes the unscripted illustration of a narrative, the individual stages of which follow one another to form a pictorial continuity.

Book illustrations made their first appearance around the middle of the fifteenth century in south Germany (Augsburg, Nuremberg, Basle, etc.), where the art of book-printing was born. Their subsequent development is closely linked with the technical development of book-printing. Whereas in the oldest books, the block-books, script and picture were cut from one and the same wood block, printing with movable type made the illustrations less dependent on the script and they were frequently printed separately. This led to a separation in the editorial field: the drawings for the illustrations were in many cases supplied by artists and executed by woodcutters or, from the middle of the sixteenth century, by copper-engravers. As these drawings were designed for immediate use, few of them have survived. But so many traditional, richly-illustrated books have been preserved that one can follow the thematic and formal development of the illustrations. Michael Wolgemut is the first artist of note who drew for illustration. But it was Dürer's drawings, together with those of the elder Holbein and the elder Cranach, mostly Bible illustrations, that inspired illustrators throughout the sixteenth century.

From the late fifteenth century onwards a significant style of illustration developed in Italy, aimed primarily at a humanistically cultured public. Therefore it had not only to find new themes but also to give them a new treatment. Botticelli's drawings for Dante's *Divine Comedy* provide an interesting example of this new approach, although the type of illustrations remained traditional: the continuous, literal illustrations of the text occupied the pages opposite the relevant text. The illustration of Canto 31 of the 'Purgatory' *(Ill. 38)*, beginning in the bottom right-hand corner, proceeds to cover the entire page. Dante appears five times. His first appearance is on this side of the river Euboe with the Roman poet Statius, then he is shown attempting to cross the river, up to his neck in the water, while Matelda, who must be regarded as the symbol of active life, glides over the waves 'light as a weaver's shuttle'. Beside her, the incarnation of human reason, stands Virgil. According to the story, Matelda dips Dante's head under water and finally, brought to the bank, he is received by the four cardinal virtues who lead him to the triumphal chariot drawn by a griffin. The main episode depicted in the illustration is the triumphal procession of the Church, which is led by the twenty-four elders. The four worldly virtues (Wisdom, Temperance, Justice and Fortitude) hover about the poet, while the three spiritual virtues (Faith, Hope and Charity) dance around in front of the chariot. The seven bands in the heavens, the seven lights – symbols for the seven gifts of the Holy Spirit and the seven sacraments – are linked to the griffin, the symbol for Christ, which draws the triumphal chariot of the Church. In the chariot sits Beatrice, incarnation of divine wisdom, and the procession is accompanied by the symbols of the four evangelists. Behind the chariot walk the apostle princes, Peter and Paul, the four fathers of the Church (Gregory, Jerome, Augustine and Ambrose) and bringing up the rear, 'sleeping albeit with thoughtful countenance', John the Evangelist. The pictorial narrative does not follow a simple sequence but highlights the more significant episodes, while the remaining scenes form a less prominent part of the composition.

Italy's contribution to book illustration consists primarily in the tectonic embellishment of the printed page with an infinite variety of architectural and decorative motifs taken from antiquity and interspersed with allegorical figures. This rigidly disciplined array of motifs, which serves to frame the text, became particularly common on title-pages, which for the first time acquired artistic status. This Italian system of decoration had a major influence on German book illustration in the sixteenth century (Holbein the Younger amongst others) and was introduced into France by Geoffroy Tory; to begin with, however, it made little impact. In the latter part of the sixteenth century book illustration was reduced to a mere form of craftsmanship without any artistic merit. The illustration becomes little more than a supplement; the separation of the printed from the illustrated page left ample scope for a more or less arbitrary choice of illustrations.

The seventeenth century with its encyclopaedic interest brought a greater demand for drawings for illustration. Apart from the title-page drawings, which were frequently on a generous scale, no single, specific form of illustration emerged. The picture which accompanied the text and still more the picture-books on religious, mythological, archaeological, historical and natural science subjects, which

were enjoying widespread popularity, drew mainly on formally self-contained and largely autonomous drawings, which were then transposed by copper-engravers. The drawings for the *Breviarium Romanum* by Rubens, like so many of his works, were translated into book form by engravers he himself had trained. The same is true of most of the portraits which Van Dyck drew for his *Iconographie (Ill. 5)*; some of them, on the other hand, he etched himself.

Another artist who worked mainly on illustrations which he etched himself is Jacques Callot, in whose drawings and sketchbooks all sorts of familiar themes are treated in an almost cryptographic style of great virtuosity *(Ill. 26)*. The figures for a kind of textbook on drawing, *Capricci di varie figure*, with sketches of soldiers, beggars, cripples and actors in the Italian comedy reveal a delicate treatment of light and shade which had many imitators and even influenced Rembrandt. Callot's style of drawing was adopted in France by Nicolas Cochin and in Italy with such fidelity by Stefano della Bella that their drawings were frequently mistaken for one another.

Although book production in Holland in the seventeenth century was extensive and the demand for illustrations correspondingly large, the outstanding draughtsman of the epoch, Rembrandt, made only a few drawings specifically for illustration. On the other hand, his Old Testament scenes in particular are nearer to the spirit and substance of biblical history, than many traditional Bible illustrations *(Ill. 45)*. An artist who is much more important as an illustrator than as a portrait and animal painter is the Englishman Francis Barlow (1626–1702), whose original drawings to illustrate Aesop's *Fables* (British Museum, London, and Ashmolean Museum, Oxford) are of as high quality as any in the seventeenth century.

The eighteenth century saw the re-emergence of a distinctive style of illustration. In France particularly bibliophiles' editions were published with full-page scenic illustrations based on sketches by outstanding painters and draughtsmen. But the character of the book page was conditioned even more by the small pictures interpolated in the text, the top and tail of the chapter *(en tête* and *cul de lampe)*, which were also separately designed. Among the illustrators are François Boucher, Hubert Gravelot, Charles Nicolas Cochin the Younger, Jean-Marie Moreau the Younger, as well as Charles-

IX PAUL CÉZANNE (Aix-en-Provence 1839–1906)

Chateau-noir. Pencil and watercolour, 1895–1900. 360:526 mm. Boymans–Van Beuningen Museum, Rotterdam. Venturi 1034.

Cézanne renders space and volume in his pictures by giving density to the areas that border the contours. Line is frequently replaced by contrapuntal hatching or a conjunction of different colours, which thus reverse their traditional function in drawing

Louis Coypel and Charles Eisen, whose small, delicately toned drawings in soft graphite made a particular impact in Germany. In Berlin Daniel Chodowiecki drew hundreds of illustrations for both classical and contemporary authors. The courtly scenes drawn by Jean-Baptiste Oudry introduced a note of grandeur into illustration, which is also present in his illustrations of La Fontaine's *Fables*, which were drawn in 1743 but appeared only twenty years later.

Characteristic of Italian book illustration was that it remains self-contained. Here too the original sketches are by such famous artists as Piazzetta and Fontebasso. In his *Capricci* engravings Tiepolo adopted the themes from Callot's illustrations and also much of his style. There is something leisurely in his manner of drawing and a painterly quality in his line texture that was to inspire no less an artist than Francisco de Goya, undoubtedly the outstanding draughtsman at the turn of the eighteenth and nineteenth centuries. The pictures in which he engaged in social criticism were also influenced by the work of the English artists William Hogarth, Thomas Rowlandson and James Gillray.

Towards the end of the eighteenth century the Englishman William Blake introduced a completely new type of book illustration. A printing process which he himself had developed enabled him to print in one single process the books which he himself had written and illustrated: the unity of script and picture in one uniform design was hereby restored. Blake's example is still followed today.

The classical artists favoured a linear style of illustration, which took an extreme form in the purely linear contour drawings of John Flaxman (Ill. p. 82). This type of illustration continued with the romantics and the Nazarenes. The calligraphic pen drawings of Moritz von Schwind and Ludwig Richter for fairy tales and sagas were the models for German illustrators throughout the nineteenth century. The English Pre-Raphaelite illustrators also fall back on the simple tectonic, predominantly graphic style of the Renaissance. Their ideal, which was to revive the artistic unity of book production, was given a fresh impetus, particularly by the illustrators of the Kelmscott Press (Walter Crane, Edward Burne-Jones) founded by William Morris. Aubrey Beardsley, who was only loosely associated with these artists, had a lasting influence on the illustration work of Art Nouveau. The delicate linearity of his strokes combines decorative ornamentalism and lively movement (Ill. p. 81), producing a fantastic network of lines or sharply contrasting areas of white and black, which are ideally suited to drawing in the flat.

In France, Honoré Daumier set a pattern which was followed long after his lifetime, a pattern which emanated not only from the breadth of his treatment, which provided scope for the chalk of the lithograph, but also from his impulsive style of illustration (by contrast with the 'objective' elegance of form preferred in Germany) which highlighted characteristic features to the point of caricature. Following in his footsteps, Gustave Doré went beyond a mere pictorial presentation of the written word to achieve a more or less independent interpretation and a picture which stands by itself. Similarly Menzel's illustrations for the *History of Frederick the Great* have an inherent greatness that raises them above mere comment on a text, and Slevogt's *Leatherstocking* drawings imbue the story with his subjective sense of form.

The picture-story in satirical and humorous periodicals developed a style of drawing entirely its own. The constantly recurring, stereotyped and caricatured figures, which were developed in the stories of Alfred Schrödter or Wilhelm Busch as pure line drawings, are directly followed by the rubrics in the satirical periodicals which were so popular around the turn of the century, and more recently by the artistically dubious modern 'comics'.

In the twentieth century the luxury editions have acquired renewed prominence, with the illustrations playing a major part. The formal production is decided by the artist, who frequently also chooses the type, thus giving the page the unity of an illustrated manuscript. Practically all traditional types of illustration continue to be employed. Alfred Kubin, George Grosz, Ernst Barlach and Käthe Kollwitz are all primarily draughtsmen with markedly illustrative tendencies, even where there is no text or in isolated drawings. Almost all the artists of the École de Paris seized the opportunity to express their conception of form in the specialized field of book illustration (Chagall, Dufy, Matisse, Braque, Picasso).

AUBREY BEARDSLEY (Brighton 1872–98 Mentone)
Apollo. Pen over pencil, 180:152 mm.
Beardsley's drawings with their strong contrast of black and white and their clear, curving lines
have become models for illustrators since the time of Art Nouveau

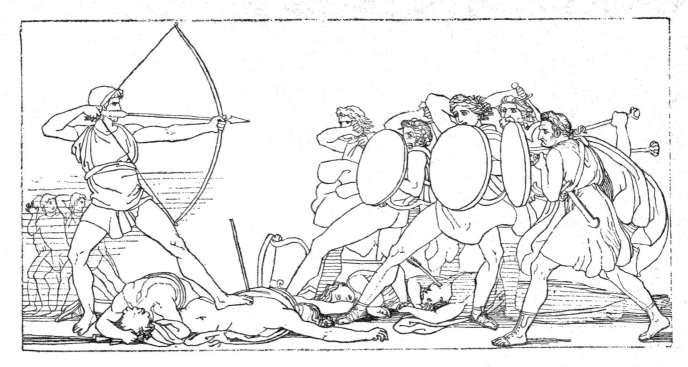

JOHN FLAXMAN (York 1755–1826 London) *Odysseus slays the suitors*. Pencil, 168:325 mm. Art Institute, Chicago. Illustration for Homer's *Odyssey*, Canto XXII. Pure line drawing with a relief-like composition was typical of the neoclassical sculptors. Flaxman also worked as an illustrator

Sculptural Drawings

Drawings by sculptors and sculptural drawings are two different things. The former, products of a dual talent, are independent expressions in a 'foreign' material, while the latter are working drawings performing a vicarious function. As the sculptor's objective is a three-dimensional sculpture, drawing with its reduction of the object to line and two dimensions represents, strictly speaking, a deviation. In the formal preparation of his work the sculptor can dispense more easily with drawings than any other artist. The preparatory models for a sculptural work which correspond to the sketch or study are the *bozzetto*, the small plastic 'rough', which can serve as a model for the final work, and – like the cartoon – the full-size model in malleable material, which can still be modified.

As in wall painting and in early panel painting so too in sculpture (though not in molten plastics) one finds the phenomenon of the drawing 'lost'

in the immediate process of creation. Before work begins on a block, the main contours are drawn on the outer faces of the block. But, unlike a sketch on a wall or panel which can simply be painted over, the contours drawn on a block literally disappear.

The earliest known sculptural drawings are probably to be found in the collections in Orvieto, Berlin and London. Together they represent the design of a chancel, which was produced between about 1350 and 1360 for the cathedral at Orvieto. Characteristic features are the clear delineation of the contours, the precise reproduction of fillet and fold, the detail of the fluted columns and the absence of any painterly expedients. This strictly linear type of drawing predominated until the sixteenth century, particularly north of the Alps, for contract designs and full-size drawings. Of special interest are the designs for the tomb of Maximilian at Innsbruck (Kupferstichkabinett, Dresden, and Albertina, Vienna), which were

82

partly the work of painters (Dürer, Amberger, Sesselschreiber), and the designs for the tomb of Sebaldus in Nuremberg by Peter Vischer the Elder (Albertina, Vienna) and Hermann Vischer (Louvre, Paris). As regards designs for altarpieces, it is often impossible to tell from the stereotyped style of drawing whether they were intended for sculptures, reliefs or paintings. On the other hand, drawings with a black background which brings the subject into sharp relief can fairly safely be associated with sculpture; examples are Antonio Pollaiuolo's design for an equestrian statue of Francesco Sforza in Munich (Staatliche Graphische Sammlung) and Hans Burgkmair's design for an equestrian statue of the Emperor Maximilian (Albertina, Vienna).

There is a strong painterly element in the Italian Renaissance artists' drawings for sculpture. Ghiberti's studies for a *Flagellation of Christ* in the Albertina, which were done in connection with the relief for the north door of the Baptistry in Florence, have short, searching lines, which merge into the firm contour and give the impression of a moving surface. Leonardo, in his studies for the Sforza memorial, also used soft, red chalk .Michelangelo, as it were, walked round his sculpture, drawing it from various sides. The convex and the concave are depicted with hatched shading, which at the intersections are reminiscent of chisel marks.

In Michelangelo's drawings the difference between a sculptural drawing and an independent drawing by a sculptor is at once apparent. The drawing for the *Madonna of Bruges* (Ill. right) concentrates entirely on the contours, while the body of the drawing is extremely economical, merely emphasizing certain features, such as the line of the clavicle, which were of special interest to the sculptor. The woman's head in Oxford (Plate X), on the other hand, is very carefully modelled with powerful, broad, parallel hatching for the shading, as though the unplanned execution should be transferred to the drawing.

The relatively few remaining sculptors' drawings from the Renaissance show a marked duality of character: the drawings themselves were regarded as complete since the formal aims of the draughtsman had been achieved; at the same time, as far as the plastic work is concerned, these sketches are only preparatory drawings.

In baroque sculptors' drawings, despite their much more painterly conception and the frequent

MICHELANGELO BUONARROTI
(Caprese 1475–1564 Rome)
Sketch for the *Madonna of Bruges* (detail). Pen, *c.* 1503. British Museum, London. Dussler 162.
Monumental sculptor's drawing, in which the staccato use of the pen seems to suggest the marble block and the chisel

83

use of the brush, the linear framework which circumscribes the mass of the body also predominates. Bernini's drawings are particularly instructive. They were frequently done in rough with soft materials such as red chalk or brush, which gives them something of the quality of paintings. But as the artist worked on them, they became more linear and the hard pen became more prominent *(Ill. 34)*. The strong chiaroscuro effects serve not so much to clarify the modelling of concrete bodily forms as to transfer the mass of the figure *per se* to the flat surface as an almost tangible form. But however much painterly skill they display, drawings when made with sculpture in view always lack depth, and in that respect they are fundamentally different from painters' drawings. This is even true of such decorative works as Pozzo's drawings for a reredos *(Ill. 35)*. Here the three-dimensional architectural features such as steps and treads are depicted in the style of an architectonic plan and the individual plastic forms look like pieces of stage scenery. Ignaz Günther's drawings are also singularly lacking in depth, and he again had recourse to a dark background in order to model his figures and groups of figures. Yet in their style of drawing and in their methodical treatment of detail, the late baroque sculptors' drawings come very close to painters' drawings and often create the impression of having been drawn from existing works of sculpture.

Abstraction, which is a characteristic feature of sculptors' drawings, is most apparent in the studies and drawings of the classicists. By contrast with earlier periods, throughout the nineteenth century drawing remained an important expression of artistic development for the sculptor. In a monument-conscious century, when the finishing process was mechanized to a degree of impersonal, technical perfection, drawings assumed even greater significance as expressions of artistic creation. At the same time more and more value was attached to the unfinished work, to the sketch. Even the sculptor's drawing acquired the aesthetic value of an independent artistic expression. And yet the essential differences from the painter's drawing – stress on contour, on bodily volume, and lack of depth – remained. When Rodin washed his sketches with an ochre tint or did them entirely with a brush, he achieved not so much a painterly effect of shadow as an impression of compact masses.

As distinct from sculptors' drawings, which are associated with a work of sculpture, whether as a form of preparation and clarification or simply because the artist is thinking in three-dimensional terms, the number of independent drawings by sculptors grows steadily in the twentieth century. Artistic expression brushes aside formal frontiers. It is no longer bound by this or that particular technique. Just as more and more painters also turn to sculpture, so there is now hardly a sculptor who does not try his hand at other forms of art.

Naturally these artists carry their formal conceptions over into the other media. For example, a characteristic feature of Henry Moore's pictures of the London underground during the Blitz *(Ill. 37)*, which give an impression of depth far beyond that of a sculptor's drawing, and also of his sculptures, are the voluminous, rounded bodies and the counterpoise of interior and exterior, of vault and cavity. As Alberto Giacometti in his sculptures breaks up the firm contours and, as it were, dovetails them into the environment, similarly, in his drawings, he creates an impression of three-dimensional space and achieves the same intangible link between the contours and the surrounding environment by a hatch-like repetition of certain pencil lines and by rubbing others – a method, incidentally, which Rodin had also employed.

X Michelangelo Buonarroti (Caprese 1475–1564 Rome)
Head of a woman. Red chalk, *c.* 1520. 166:206 mm. Ashmolean Museum, Oxford. Frey 172b; Dussler 342. Reproduction original size.
This red chalk drawing can be regarded as one of those presentation sheets to which Vasari refers as 'teste divine'. Early example of an obvious connoisseur's and collector's drawing

Architectural Drawings

Architectural drawing, even more than the sculptor's drawing, occupies a special position. Here again one must distinguish between the independent drawing by an architect, the spontaneous building design which is an end-product in itself, and the strictly practical, working drawing of a plan without any artistic aspiration. By contrast with painting and especially sculpture, which can dispense with a preparatory drawing, the master-builder can only realize his project if he has several drawings, most of them geometrically constructed, which give the ground-plan and elevation of the building to an exact scale but without providing a view in depth. Although there are special graphic formulations which betray the identity of the author, these geometrical drawings are still impersonal. The artistic evolution of a work of architecture is usually reflected in a series of such plans. Frequently alternative proposals are put forward to show the two sides of a symmetrically planned building with variations of form. Sometimes these are drawn on separate strips of paper which are stuck on and can be unfolded.

The oldest surviving plan does not really fall into the category of precise working drawings, as it was not intended for immediate practical application and therefore was not drawn to scale. It is a plan of the monastery of St Gallen which was drawn on parchment about the year 820. This unique document of medieval building technique depicts the ideal site for a spacious monastery with a succession of adjoining buildings and gardens but with no indication that any of the buildings should have a particular character. On the other hand, the Gothic projections and working designs, the largest collection of which is in the Kupferstichkabinett of the Vienna Akademie, were clearly designed for actual use. Many of these working drawings for individual architectural features are full-size and could be directly converted to the stone. Large sections of the construction were often drawn on the ground or on a wall near the site, thereby serving the same purpose as a cartoon. These early Gothic architectural drawings avoid perspective and their orthogonal presentation of buildings has remained normal practice to this day.

Architectural free sketches and designs more closely resemble other artistic drawings, both in technique and appearance, especially since perspective drawing also became widespread in the Renaissance, thus providing a self-contained picture. In the case of extensive building complexes the central perspective view is frequently replaced by a bird's-eye view and the interior is presented in the distorted form of a wide-angle view. Apart from the concrete designs for specific building projects, idealistic designs already made their first appearance in the early Renaissance period. Though practicable, they were not originally designed for practical use. Among these are most of the school and pattern drawings, which, beginning with Alberti, played an important part in works on architectural theory. Then there were plans for municipal buildings and fortifications, in which Leonardo da Vinci was greatly interested and which also occupy a prominent place in Dürer's work. Finally we find the fantastic but nonetheless realistically conceived designs of the classicists of the revolution, such as Ledoux's spherical building.

Related to these idealistic designs and architectural fantasies are the scenographic designs, sometimes in the form of engravings, such as were produced in the sixteenth century in the Netherlands by Vredeman de Vries, followed by Joseph Furttenbach in Germany. They were intended in part for stage decorations; but their bizarre profusion of architectural style and detail also served as background for contemporary pictures. From the seventeenth century onwards, stage decorations become an increasingly conspicuous feature of architectural drawings, forming a special category which combined both architecture and decoration in landscape pictures (Galli-Bibiena family).

But from the seventeenth century onwards even the sober, professional architectural drawing in its strictly concrete form becomes more and more pictorial. The design itself was embellished with landscape and figures, as in the drawings of Israel Silvestre in France and particularly in Johann Bernhard Fischer von Erlach's *Codex Montenuovo* in the Albertina and the drawings for his *Entwurf einer historischen Architektur* (Zagreb, Linz, Salzburg). These drawings give a self-contained, pictorial impression reminiscent of the drawn 'vedute'. Architectonic drawings, particularly in the eighteenth century, are often so painterly and ornamental in their presentation, so enlivened by decorative figures and entire scenes that they have all the appearance of independent works with an intrinsic value of their own. The transition from the architectural drawing to the painter's drawing was completed in Piranesi's works, which are strongly influenced by scenography and the romantic landscapes with ruins *(Ill. 28)*.

In the nineteenth century the architectural drawing again concentrated more on a precise, linear style of presentation, which did not, however, entirely exclude the pictorial element in the style of the 'veduta'. Since the beginning of the twentieth century, however, increasing prominence has been given to the free, sketch-like notation of an architectonic idea. Designs for buildings, bringing out certain general features and omitting all detail, are largely reduced to 'cyphers', translating structural and functional ideas into unorthodox, graphic formulas (Le Corbusier). In chosing the title *Bach Cantata* for his architectural sketches, Erich Mendelsohn consciously created an association with music. And in architectural drawings – without prejudice to the validity and necessity of precise plans for specific building projects – the architect's 'handwriting' acquires a value of its own as an expression of artistic creativeness, in keeping with the general trend towards independent drawings.

Quite apart from their purely architectural significance, the drawings of variously gifted or universal artists have distinct calligraphic qualities. Altdorfer's architectural drawings, for all their precision, were based on principles of painting and many of them served in fact as models for pictures such as the fantastic Mannerist building in *Susanna in the bath* (drawing in Düsseldorf, picture in Munich). Michelangelo's fundamentally sculptural approach also conditioned his architectural drawings.

Similarly, Bernini's drawings are characteristic of a sculptor, and a feature of Pozzo's drawings is their close relationship with scenography *(Ill. 35)*.

A special form of architectural drawing is the picture which for archaeological, topographical or simple, practical reasons (where the building in question is to be converted or extended), depicts the building in its existing state. Drawings of this kind, which by their very nature are objective and impersonal, may acquire great historical value if they portray buildings which have since disappeared or been altered, or if they are the work of artists whose personal imprint has artistic merit. The Roman sketchbooks of the architect Giuliano da Sangallo (1445–1516) combine both elements, as do Heemskerck's (1498–1574) drawings of ancient ruins and Roman buildings, of which the drawings of the new St Peter's in Rome which was built over the early Christian church are particularly valuable. The same applies to the many other painters' drawings of the sixteenth and seventeenth centuries with architectonic motifs. The clear, unpretentious drawings of the architectural painter Pieter J. Saenredam have a unique fascination, while Piranesi's Roman 'vedute' combine baroque pathos with the romantic love of ruins. Despite their detailed reproduction of nature, the 'vedute' of the Venetians Antonio Canaletto, Bernardo Bellotto and Francesco Guardi have distinct painterly qualities. A large number of the drawings made by itinerant artists and dilettantes are pictures of buildings, although frequently the artist lapsed into landscape drawing. The more the artist's personal imprint asserts itself over simple reproduction, the nearer the final work is to independent drawing, and Erich Mendelsohn's architectural drawings are an example of this (Ill. below).

ERICH MENDELSOHN (Allenstein, East Prussia 1887–1953 San Francisco) Sketch of the Schocken department store, Stuttgart. Brush and Indian ink, 1926. Louise Mendelsohn collection, San Francisco. Not a few of Mendelsohn's architectural sketches are graphic 'symbols' with specific rules of harmony

30 BACCIO BANDINELLI (Florence c. 1488–1559/60)
Laocoon. Pen and ink, 417:255 mm. Uffizi, Florence.
The antique Laocoon group, which was found in the Baths of Titus in Rome in 1506, was regarded as the epitome of classical art and was closely studied, especially by sculptors and pupils of the Michelangelo school. This drawing in large format with its sure and powerful lines and its stress on muscle formation is characteristic of Bandinelli's work. The ink, which must have been originally black but has become brown, has caused considerable damage to the paper.

31 PETER PAUL RUBENS (Siegen 1577–1640 Antwerp)
Angel pointing upwards. Detail from a copy of a fresco by Paris Bordone, *St Liberale with an angel*. Watercolour over black chalk and red ochre, 399:176 mm. Louvre, Paris. Glück–Haberditzl 1.
In his studies from earlier masters Rubens copied their compositions but also their style of painting so closely that it is sometimes difficult to identify his work with certainty.

32 TIZIANO VECELLIO known as TITIAN
(Pieve di Cadore 1487–1576 Venice)
Two kneeling boys in a landscape. Pen in bistre, 236:213 mm. Albertina, Vienna. Cat. I. 38. Hadeln 7; Tietze 1970.
This drawing was made in two distinct stages. After the two boys had been drawn with only a vague background, the landscape was added. The difference in tone and firmness of line were so striking that another artist was thought to have completed the picture. This independent drawing by Titian, who as a rule only drew preparatory to painting, has passed through a number of collections, which left their stamps at the bottom of the drawing.

33 ANTOINE WATTEAU
(Valenciennes 1684–1721 Nogent-sur-Marne)
Two kneeling boys in a landscape. Red chalk, 234:233 mm. Louvre, Paris. Parker Mathey 438.
Copy of Titian's drawing *(Ill. 32)*.
Watteau did much of his drawing from other works and he preserved and revised them like his nature studies. He may have seen Titian's drawing in the Crozat Collection. Both drawings then found their way into Mariette's possession.

34 GIOVANNI LORENZO BERNINI
(Naples 1598–1680 Rome)
Sketch sheet. Pen and ink over pencil and red chalk,
1631. 265:326 mm. Albertina, Vienna. Brauer–Wittkower T. 7.
The red chalk sketches for the tabernacle of St Peter in Rome were corrected again and again; the detail drawings in pencil and pen, which are on a larger scale, were more carefully done.

35 ANDREA DEL POZZO (Rome 1642–1709 Vienna)
Altar design. Pen and brush over pencil drawing, grey wash, 407:279 mm. Uffizi, Florence.
By contrast with the page from Bernini's sketchbook, on which the variants are placed side by side, enabling us to follow the evolution of the final drawing, Pozzo's drawing is conceived like a baroque ornament, showing one side fully completed, the other merely sketched in. This drawing, despite its practical purpose, becomes an aesthetic composition enlivened with human figures who also serve to indicate scale.

36 ALBERTO GIACOMETTI (Stampa 1901–66 Chur)
Seated man. Pencil, 1953. 504:327 mm. Wallraf-Richartz-Museum, Cologne.
Both in his sculptures and in his drawings Giacometti deliberately avoided the firm outline. The absence of detail in his sculptures is echoed in the parallel repetitions of lines and the rubbing out of contours. In this way figure and background are seen to merge.

37 HENRY MOORE (Castlefort, Yorkshire, 1898)
Underground shelter in Tilbury. Pen and ink with watercolour, 1941. 410:375 mm. Tate Gallery, London. Read 183.
Henry Moore also regards the drawing not as a faithful representation of sculpture but a formal medium of its own, which, though related to his sculpture, translates the convex and concave of his bodies into two-dimensional terms by means of flowing lines.

38 SANDRO BOTTICELLI (Florence 1444/45–1510)
Illustration to Dante. Pen and ink over soft metal stylus on parchment, 324:476 mm. Kupferstichkabinett, Staatliche Museen, Berlin (East).
Literal illustration of the text on the facing page *(Purgatory, Canto 31)*.
In this 'strip' presentation of the story, Dante appears five times. The delicate, strictly linear, flat treatment was designed for painting with body colours. The miniature 'layout' produces the effect of an independent drawing.

30

31

32

33

34

35

36

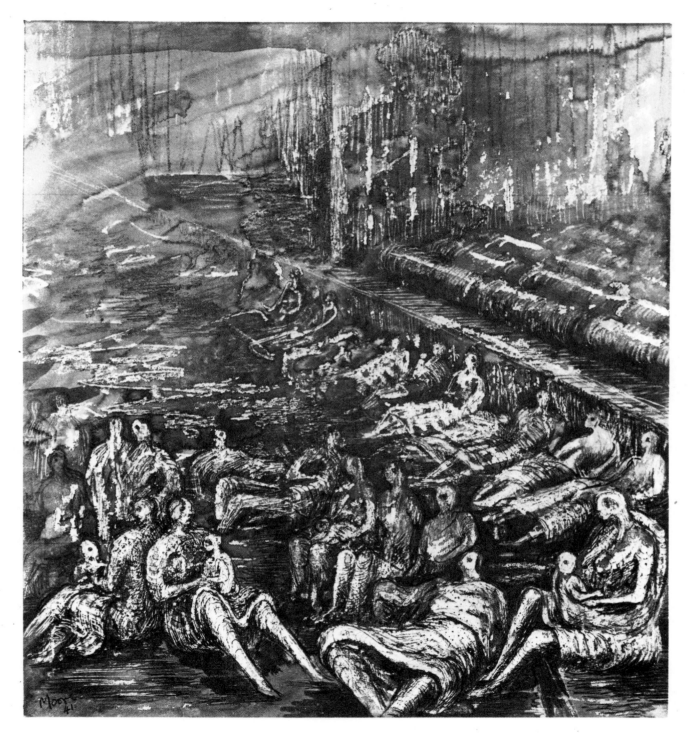

37

31

38

The Independent Drawing

The tradition of the independent drawing began in the fifteenth century in Italy. Although the essentially functional character of many early drawings, for example, those in the broad margins or empty pages of codices, is not always immediately apparent, one can nevertheless assume that it 'is the primary motive for a work or is the primary consequence of such a work or again forms a direct link between one work and another or finally represents a substantial part of a work which is completed or in process of completion' (Degenhart). Drawing as an end in itself may well be older than tradition makes it out to be, but it is only with the dawn of the Renaissance that the essential features of the independent drawing begin to emerge more and more clearly. The artistic process of the search for form, which first becomes apparent in the series of drawings by Italian artists in the fifteenth century, differs fundamentally both from the medieval concept of the 'simile', in other words the closest possible reproduction of a pattern, and from the formally self-contained drawing which developed from this process in the Netherlands and Germany. The rough drawing, 'artistic in conception and at least in part creative', marks a significant step towards realizing the main criterion of the independent drawing: 'to be an expression of the creative, artistic spirit' (Degenhart).

The intellectual and material ties with a particular work of art are largely broken by the rough drawing; as soon as a drawing is entirely spontaneous, these ties are broken altogether.

As the artist became more and more conscious of the subjective element in artistic creation, the rough drawing became more and more independent. And as the sketch came to acquire recognition as an artistic, 'calligraphic', individual expression, the dividing line between 'functional' and independent drawing, which was already fluid, became completely blurred and purely subjective. This fundamental change of approach set in as early as the sixteenth century. For more recent and present times, the old concepts of preparatory and completed, of functional and independent drawing are, by and large, no longer applicable. Today the sketch-like, so-called 'open' style of drawing may be employed for practice, notation or for sketching, or it may equally well be a consciously adopted style. But even in the case of drawings which are formally and pictorially complete it is not always easy to distinguish between the exact, preliminary drawing, for example for a graphic print, and the independent composition. In many instances the distinction between a detail study, a rough drawing or a preliminary drawing can only be made according to whether the final work was completed and can be identified; so the criterion is often a purely material one. On the other hand, works which were initially independent drawings can later be used, either wholly or in part, as models and thus be rated as preliminary drawings.

The ability to judge whether a drawing is to be defined as independent or functional calls in most cases for an individual enquiry into the period and the artist and for a sense of the historical background. The works of artists, who have concentrated entirely or even largely on drawing, must be judged differently from drawings by painters, sculptors or architects. And drawings by predominantly graphic artists again must be seen in relation to their graphic work; the drawings of Jacques Callot (1592–1653), Stefano della Bella (1610–64) or Daniel Chodowiecki (1726–1801), for example, are essential to their engravings, even when no direct relationship is apparent. Pictorially complete drawings are more likely to have some association with plans for prints than rough sketches. And the same is true of single sheets by artists who were mainly engaged on illustration. Drawings not directly linked with a text may be regarded as independent works, whereas illustrations, though as drawings they are an end in themselves, are nevertheless functional in relation to the text. On the other hand, sketches by artists who concentrated entirely on drawing, such as Raymond La Fage (1656–90), who was hailed as a new Michelangelo, are an end in themselves.

In the fifteenth century the individual 'calligraphy' of the artist was still overshadowed by the style of the period, with its contours drawn in thin, precise and long, sweeping strokes. The lines of the detail drawing are also clear, almost always unbroken and – especially in the north – ornamental. A good example of this particular style is a drawing by Master ES of a distinguished lady – it is not clear whether she is a saint, probably St Catherine, or a secular celebrity. This drawing does not give the impression of being tied to any subsequent work (Ill. 39). And yet the short, curled strokes of the modelling suggest a copperengraving. Examples of drawings which show a more markedly independent tendency are some of the works of Martin Schongauer, who adopted the linear elegance of the great Dutch masters but adapted it freely to an accentuated, minutely-detailed linear pattern of his own. Most compositions by Jan van Eyck (c. 1390–1441) or Rogier van der Weyden (c. 1400–64), however, have only survived in copies. The Dutch style of drawing is also reflected in Albrecht Dürer's first self-portrait (Ill. 1). The thin lines of the silverpoint drawing are repeated and reinforced in the contours and the main lines of the detail-drawing and the modelling is done with fine, evenly spaced lines reminiscent of goldsmiths' work. This drawing, the highly conscious self-portrait of a boy in a style peculiar to the end of the Middle Ages, which may have been a test of skill and was later extensively annotated by Dürer himself, is of great historical value. The predominantly flat linear style of drawing continued north of the Alps; its basic components persistently reasserted themselves.

Amongst the earliest independent drawings from Italy are certain pages in the sketchbooks of Jacopo Bellini (c. 1400–70) such as the pictorially self-contained landscape with St Christopher (Louvre, Paris); its calligraphic line structure, however, was still in conformity with the style of the period. In Antonio Pollaiuolo's pen drawing of prisoners before a judge (British Museum, London), the modelling of the figures is also subordinated to the flatness of the line, and its silhouette effect is accentuated by the dark background. This linear style of drawing continued until the late fifteenth century, as is shown by Leonardo's uncompleted drawing of a kneeling Madonna (Plate V) and Botticelli's illustrations of Dante (Ill. 38). Neither of these, on the other hand, is an independent drawing.

But in the fifteenth century the Italian Renaissance drawings already showed a tendency to concentrate more on plastic qualities and to adopt a freer, more painterly approach to contours. The central Italian, Tuscan drawings are almost all directly linked with larger works. The strokes are clear and thin and concentrate on the essential physical features; the plasticity is underlined by clearly-defined groups of hatching. In north Italy, particularly in Venice, the optical approach predominated. Regular and often uninterrupted lines, flat but firm contours and overlapping hatching produce a painterly impression. This style of drawing is in keeping with the Venetian leaning towards scenic presentation and heightens the pictorial effect of the drawings.

In the sixteenth century drawing rapidly gained in importance and in Germany and Holland achieved a degree of independence hitherto unknown as a self-contained work of pictorial art. The outstanding artistic personality is Albrecht Dürer who, within a few years, starting from the thin lines and painstaking technique of the engraver, explored all the possibilities of realistic presentation until he achieved a relaxed yet commanding style of his own; for more than a generation his style remained a model.

Dürer's method of drawing, like that of the sixteenth century as a whole, is based on line. One resolute stroke outlines the major forms with smooth fluency. Linear repetitions, which can be intensified to thick parallel hatchings, serve to reinforce the curves or the solidity of the angles. By means of small, uniform hooks and curls, which produce a somewhat brittle effect, the modelling of detail, the rounding of the figures, the folds in clothes, the branches of trees and bushes, the hide of animals, are translated as graphic 'symbols'. Loose, thick layers of hatching, most of them uniformly covering fairly large areas, broken where some minute point of detail requires it or overlapping, and heavy cross-hatching in the curves heighten the three-dimensional impression. The varying density of the strokes produces the effects of light and shade. Precision of detail and compact form give clarity to the foreground, while vague suggestion, vanishing contours and sketchy detail give the background its atmosphere. By subtle tonal effects the illusion of a multiplicity of single strokes is created, and brush and chalk are also employed to give a linear rather than a planar effect. The animation of the whole drawing and the differentiation of its individual components are largely the result of the varying breadth of the line and of the personal, calligraphic imprint of the artist inherent in every stroke. His individual studies, landscapes, portraits and scenic compositions gain increasingly in artistic merit. His *Madonna with the many animals* (Plate IV) combines all the requirements of a devotional picture with the immediate freshness of a coloured pen drawing; it includes in one and the same richly varied drawing a profusion of nature studies of plants and animals, a picture of the Madonna and a genre-style portrayal of biblical episodes in the remote landscape. Albrecht Altdorfer's *Christ on the Mount of Olives* (*Ill. 40*; the Dürer monogram was erroneously added later), with its landscape inspired by the forests of the Danube valley and the Alpine peaks, also acquires character of its own by the painterly effect of a pen drawing with white highlights on coloured paper. Using purely graphic means, Hans Baldung Grien in his *St Christopher* manages to produce a remarkable three-dimensional impression. On the tinted paper the light areas were drawn in white, the darker ones in black with equal emphasis, thus breaking through the two-dimensional barrier of the drawing (Plate XI). Just as these three works must rank as small-

XI HANS BALDUNG known as GRIEN (Swabian Gmünd (?) 1484/85–1545 Strasbourg) ▶
St Christopher. Pen in black and white on greenish-light brown grounded paper, 281:192 mm. Staatliche Kunsthalle, Karlsruhe. Koch 35.
Chiaroscuro drawing with equal application of black and white. The areas of light and shade complement one another, giving this picture on tinted paper great painterly qualities despite the distintly graphic and linear style of drawing

scale pictures, many drawings by German and Dutch artists can equally be regarded as independent works; they fulfil the function of the print on a more exacting level.

South of the Alps pictorial drawings of this kind are rarer. At the beginning of the century completed pictures were produced almost exclusively in northern Italy. In general it is the rough drawing that is most common in Italy and with it an open, loose style of drawing in which the contour is invariably broken. The process of developing a figure-sketch into a self-contained drawing can be followed in Titian's *Boys kneeling in a landscape (Ill. 32)*. The landscape was added to the two figures at a later stage to complete the picture. The value attached to this composition by artists and collectors and the extent to which they considered it an independent work can be gauged from Watteau's copy *(Ill. 33)* and from the number of collectors' stamps, which show through how many large collections the Titian drawing passed.

An example of an independent drawing from central Italy is Michelangelo's *Head of a woman* (Plate X), which was very probably intended as a gift. The statuesque quality and form of this idealistic portrait distinguish it from the Renaissance portrait studies (*cf.* Holbein, Plate VI).

In no other period were all the possibilities open to the draughtsman so thoroughly explored as in the adventurous sixteenth century. The most varied techniques enjoyed equal status and determined the nature of each individual drawing. Descriptive naturalism with its wealth of detail is to be found principally in Dutch drawings (*cf.* Bruegel, *Ill. 2*; Swart, *Ill. 41*); in the Florentines one finds a more summary treatment and larger figures (*cf.* Pontormo, *Ill. 24*) together with affected graphic modelling (*cf.* Vasari, *Ill. 21*). Northern Italy remained faithful to its painting tradition and sought equivalent graphic methods in the brush drawing (*cf.* Parmigianino, *Ill. 20*); the Venetians in particular translated the optical effects of light into the language of drawing by blurring the outlines (*cf.* Tintoretto, *Ill. 22*). In addition to figure compositions, the sixteenth century also saw the emergence of single figures with allegorical, mythological or religious significance as independent drawings (Spranger, *Apollo*; *Ill. 23*). Landscape compositions began to play a great part; thanks largely to the Dutch, they achieved a status of their own. The frequent adaptation of the landscape, as seen, to the

XII Rosalba Giovanna Carriera (Venice 1675–1757) ▶
Portrait of a youth from the Leblond family. Pastel, 336:280 mm. Accademia, Venice.
By rubbing pastel crayons and mixing the colours, the pastel drawing can be made to look like a painting. The delicate clarity of the pastel made it one of the favourite media of the portrait artist, particularly in the eighteenth century

various styles of drawing leads in most of these drawings to spontaneous, independent compositions, as in so many of the pen drawings of Pieter Bruegel the Elder or in the brush drawings of Hans Bol.

These independent landscape drawings were preceded by Leonardo's scientifically-inspired landscape and storm drawings. With ingenious inventiveness he devises graphic equivalents for rock strata, cloud formations and air currents and shapes them into impressive visions, which open up new and unexpected vistas. The fact that these completely pictorial drawings are essentially nature studies, illustration drawings or even scientific schemata is entirely forgotten when one looks at the dense conglomeration of whirling circles; moreover to the modern observer it seems irrelevant.

The strong element of subjectivity in mannerism, as regards both content and form, finds its most obvious outlet in the impressive, frequently private and intimate character of the drawings, which even in material terms lacked all extravagance (*cf.* Parmigianino's brush drawing, *Ill. 20*). Virtuosity, love of experiment and an arbitrary mixture of various techniques add up to a highly individualistic, opalescent picture of draughtsmanship in the sixteenth century *(cf. Ills 12, 15, 20, 21, 22, 23, 24, 30)*.

Putting to account all the experiences of the preceding period, the seventeenth century developed a more rigorous conception of the picture as such and separated the various categories analogous to painting. The highly disciplined baroque movement, which began in Rome and Bologna and which was primarily composition conscious, also influenced drawing, from the composition sketch to the independent work. Again one finds the functional drawing prevalent among the Italians and, as a direct consequence, with Rubens and his school; whereas the Dutch, even if they spent years in Rome, attached greater importance to pictorial compactness in drawing. But common to them all is the firm, broad style of drawing with a liberal use of flat washes and the additional application of tints or colours (*cf. Ills 3, 5, 6, 17, 31, 42, 43, 44, 48*; Plates II, VIII).

The ideal, composed landscape drawing was invested with picturesque sentiment by the Brothers Carracci *(Ill. 42)* and in Claude Lorrain's drawings *(Ill. 43)* it achieves an entirely new harmony between the dark corridors of the trees and

XIII EDGAR-HILAIRE DEGAS (Paris 1834–1919)
Dancers. Pastel, 980:890 mm. Kupferstichkabinett, Staatliche Kunstsammlungen, Dresden. Lemoisne 1331.
Degas shows a superb mastery of the varied potentialities of pastel and exploits them together. A combination of flat, rubbed surfaces and accentuating lines, together with bright colour, give an impression of lightness and mobility even to the large format and create the atmosphere so cherished by the impressionists

the groups of figures on the one hand, and the broad, light landscape beyond. The pictorial approach even to the preliminary composition drawing and the nature sketch is particularly clear in the drawings of Poussin *(Ill. 44)* or Salvator Rosa *(Ill. 6)*. By contrast, Jan Asselijn's drawing *(Ill. 3)*, to which the ornamental script lends a note of finality, has a predominantly anecdotal quality. The Dutch artists as a whole had a penchant for the genre picture as well as the landscape (A. van Ostade, 1610–85; David Teniers the Younger, 1610–90). In Holland the still-life, sometimes in colour, was also a popular subject with draughtsmen (J. de Heem, 1606–84).

Rembrandt was a tireless draughtsman, who exploited all the possibilities of pencil, pen and brush with great virtuosity. Few artists have drawn so much and so effectively, and for no other artist did the drawing become such an integral part of his art. Each individual drawing is an independent work of art, even where it can also be described as a nature study or composition drawing. Rembrandt's style of drawing is always based on the dramatic contrast of light and shade. The contour is seldom completely closed and the individual stroke with its varying intensity in itself creates an effect of light and shade. The lines are relaxed and free, frequently changing direction or crossing, sometimes abruptly interrupted or dramatically reinforced by repetition; the result is a basic structure which is then completed with a brush wash, by feathering, or with dense cross-hatching. With a soft brush, broad chalk or sometimes with a reed pen whose firm strokes produce dramatic emphasis, the depths of the shadows are contrasted with the white, heightened reflections of light. As a rule the empty spaces on the paper are used to bring out effects of light and so become an integral part of the drawing. His complete mastery of every technique of draughtsmanship and his skill in depicting objects and effects of light in the graphic, monochrome medium make him one of the most important, if not the greatest, of draughtsmen *(Ill. 45;* Plate II).

In the eighteenth century the widespread interest shown by collectors enhanced the value of drawing and the status of contemporary works; even preparatory sketches and studies ranked as independent artistic expressions. Watteau's drawings, many of which were used several times as models for other compositions, have this dual distinction. Conceived as pictures and yet at the same time rough sketches, in which the artist's 'signature', so coveted by collectors, is unmistakable, they were collector's pieces for two reasons *(cf.* Plate XV). Like the soft, relaxed paintings of the period with their delicate colours, the drawings of the eighteenth century are also characterized by soft pencil work and broad lines, or in many cases by brush work alone or by coloured chalks.

Whereas true preparatory drawings and composition sketches were often confined to a clear, graphic framework as a means of setting the stage *(cf.* Troger's

JOHANN FRIEDRICH OVERBECK (Lübeck 1789–1869 Rome) *The Raising of Lazarus*. Pen, *c.* 1808.
427:548 mm. Kunstmuseum, Düsseldorf. This drawing is the 'programme piece' in which Overbeck expressed his opposition to the routine style of the contemporary academies. Deliberately
modelling himself on the art of the fifteenth century, he sought a revival of form. He included
his friend Franz Pforr and himself on the left of the picture as observers of the miracle

sketch for a roof painting, *Ill. 46*), for independent drawings the principles of the
late baroque illusionist photochromy were carried over into the techniques of
drawing. In a brush drawing that is suffused with light, Honoré Fragonard
combines the large, sentimental form of composition with a portrait study, to
produce a narrative picture *(Ill. 27)*. Pen drawings, in which the contours are
merely suggested, were enlivened with washes and sparingly-used watercolours,
while reflections of light and deep shadows subdued the surrounding lines *(cf.*

Tiepolo, *Ill. 47*; Piranesi, *Ill. 28*). The solidity of the bodies in the chalk drawings gives an impression of soft hatching (Piazzetta, *Ill. 49*), and the colour effect was enhanced, particularly in portraits, by the use of pastel crayons. The delicate colouring and the light, hazy character of the pastel stroke were a perfectly adequate substitute for painting. The Venetian artist, Rosalba Carriera, who was a brilliant exponent of this technique, found many admirers and imitators particularly in France and then throughout Europe (Plate XII).

Goya combined a preference for brush drawings and baroque composition with a range of themes that remained topical far into the nineteenth century. Dramatic contrasts of light and shade are employed to portray contemporary events and human suffering in the most expressive form. Many of his drawings were produced with a view to preparing cycles of prints and yet they cannot be regarded as straightforward preliminary drawings. The rough strokes of the reed pen and the broad technique of the brush seem hardly suitable for conversion to prints. They are to a large extent independent works, in no way inferior to his pictures, his etchings or his lithographs *(Ill. 51)*.

In the nineteenth century two fundamentally different conceptions of style developed side by side. The painterly tradition, with the loose, whirling lines, vague contours and preference for contrasts of light and shade, together with the predominance of certain themes, which began with Goya, continued with Delacroix *(cf. Ill. 52)*, Géricault and Daumier *(Ill. 53)*. The classical artists who emerged at the end of the eighteenth century adopted quite a different approach. The firm outlines, hard, sculptural modelling and restrained colouring of their pictures give fresh prominence to the linear pencil and pen drawing. In many cases a composition drawn with precision ranked in itself as an artistic achievement. Amongst those who held this view were Jacques-Louis David with his statuesque monumentality *(cf. Ill. 16)* and J. A. D. Ingres with his soft sensuality (Ill. p. 35).

The thin line drawing with a sharp pen or hard pencil is also characteristic of the romantics and especially of the Nazarenes *(cf. Ill. 4)*. The drawing as an independent work of art again acquired prominence, particularly as the portrait drawing, and experienced what was often a conscious revival of the technique and style of the fifteenth century. The 'clarity of form' in Overbeck's *Raising of Lazarus* is typical (Ill. p. 107).

XIV Pablo Picasso (Malaga 1881) ►
Head of a bearded man. Coloured crayons, 1955. 310:230. Galerie Berggruen, Paris.
Picasso picks out the head by the 'open' line structure and by using different colours for the individual contours. The distribution of the ornamental loops of colour emphasizes the decorative, two-dimensional effect of the portrait

Le 1ᵉʳ Janvier 1955

Since about the middle of the nineteenth century anatomy has played an increasingly important part in drawing, which has been regarded as an independent art form on a par with painting. This applies as much to works which are pictorially complete and which sometimes even resemble easel pictures in format – for example the pastels of Degas (Plate XIII), which account for by far the greater part of his creative output – as to free, open, 'unfinished' sketches.

The high degree of artistic recognition accorded to drawing is clearly reflected in the relationship between it and the pictures of the artists who can be regarded as the most important precursors and pioneers of twentieth-century art. Georges Seurat in his statically-constructed café drawings *(Ill. 54)* translates into monochrome the theory of pointillist colour dispersal. The static harmony of Cézanne's pictures finds its equivalent in his contourless drawings with 'extended' hatching and lightly toned brush-marks, which enclose the various objects (Plate IX). He put various minute hatches, which vary both in direction and in thickness, close together, and produced physical and spatial effects from the pure flatness of the drawing by exploiting their diverse qualities of light and shade. The dynamic line of Van Gogh's reed pen drawings *(Ill. 57)* again is in complete conformity with the expressively coloured brushwork in his pictures.

In the twentieth century, draughtsmanship as such commands a great deal of interest among artists, who are now more concerned with form than content. The primary element of drawing, the monochrome line in the flat, again emerges in sharper contrast to the colour technique of the watercolour, which is also evaluated on its own merits. The modern drawings are primarily 'graphic', although here too all the intermediary stages must be taken into account. The abandonment of the illusionist type of picture has given fresh prominence to the line, which, as no more than a means of determining form, has acquired an intrinsic value of its own. In Klimt's drawing firm, unbroken contours with plastic qualities are used as a means of portrayal, usually of faces, in conjunction with curves which extend into the flat and are in no way bound up with the portrayal of an object, forming a free yet ornamental pattern *(Ill. 9)*. This is a fairly typical example of the independent role played by line as a direct, graphic medium of expression, a role which has been fully exploited in the art of succeeding generations, in which the object completely disappears and line becomes almost a form of seismogram.

The question of preparing and completing a drawing now becomes irrelevant, and conventional criteria are simply not applicable to drawings such as Klee's *Canal docks (Ill. 56)*, Kandinsky's compositions (Ill. p. 138) or Picasso's drawings (Ill. p. 34; Plate XIV). Drawing and painting are on an equal plane, two quite different solutions to one artistic problem. Drawing has become accepted as conclusive evidence of artistic creation.

39 MASTER ES (active Upper Rhine 1450–67)
St Catherine (?). Pen and brush in black ink with reddish tint, 286:185 mm. Stiftung Preussischer Kulturbesitz, Kupferstichkabinett, Staatliche Museen, Berlin. Reproduction slightly reduced.

The calligraphy of the thin pen strokes is in keeping not only with the Gothic tradition of draughtsmanship but also with the technique of the copperengraving, which the Master, who is known only by his initials, was one of the first to cultivate successfully.

40 ALBRECHT ALTDORFER (Regensburg? *c.* 1480–1538).
Christ on the Mount of Olives. Pen in black ink, heightened with white on red-brown grounded paper, 1509. 210:157 mm. Stiftung Preussischer Kulturbesitz, Kupferstichkabinett, Staatliche Museen, Berlin. Winziger 13. Reproduction in original size.

In this pictorially complete composition with its vibrant, short, curling lines, Altdorfer achieves a very lively and painterly effect, which is further enhanced by the coloured background. The 'AA 1509' originally inscribed at the top was presumably removed with forgery in mind, and a Dürer monogram with the year 1508 was inserted below.

41 JAN SWART VAN GRONINGEN
(Groningen *c.* 1500–after 1553 Antwerp (?))
Boaz discovers Ruth in the field. Pen in bistre, wash, 274:203 mm. Albertina, Vienna. Cat I, 93. Reproduction slightly reduced.

One of a series of drawings for painting on glass. As an important aid to modelling, the slow and therefore somewhat shaky pen strokes are supplemented by brush.

42 ANNIBALE CARRACCI (Bologna 1560–1609 Rome)
Landscape with bridge. Pen in bistre, wash, 175:270 mm. Gabinetto Nazionale delle Stampe, Rome.

Powerful pen strokes give solidity to a somewhat sentimental landscape composed on baroque principles. The dark shadows of the brush wash provide the necessary perspective.

43 CLAUDE GELLÉE known as LORRAIN
(Château de Chamagne 1600–82 Rome)
Landscape with tower. Pen, brush in bistre, wash, 185:300 mm. Musée du Petit Palais, Paris.

Most of the effect is achieved with brush work, the pen supplying only distant contours and delicate detail. The interchange of light and dark areas and the slightly inclined lines of the terrain lead the eye imperceptibly into the background.

44 NICOLAS POUSSIN (Villers 1594–1665 Rome)
Daphne and Apollo. Pen in bistre, wash, over black chalk, 1664. 310:430 mm. Louvre, Paris. Friedlaender–Blunt 174.

Preliminary drawing for a picture in the Louvre which was never quite completed.

Poussin combines a sublime calm in the composition of his figures with a very varied style of drawing. Within the one sheet pen and brush vie for supremacy. Whereas the brush is used to introduce perspective into the loosely-drawn pen contours of the trees and bushes, for the figures, sketched in with the brush, the pen is used to give contours and perspective.

45 REMBRANDT HARMENSZ. VAN RIJN
(Leiden 1606–69 Amsterdam)
The Prophet Jonah before the walls of Niniveh. Reed pen in bistre, wash, 1654–55. 217:173 mm. Albertina, Vienna. Benesch 950. Reproduction in original size.

Rembrandt portrays a scene from the Old Testament (Jonah 4, 5) not so much to illustrate the text ('and there made him a hut and sat under it in the shadow') as to give a visionary presentation of the prophet's anxious fears. From the deep shadows of the rough reed pen, the brush wash carries the eye to the dazzling brilliance of the unfilled spaces. A striking example of light effects in a monochrome technique.

46 PAUL TROGER (Zell, Pustertal 1698–1762 Vienna)
Allegory of Mercy. Pen in bistre, natural chalk, 202:326 mm. Albertina, Vienna. Cat. IV. 2080; Aschenbrenner 184.

Drawing for a roof painting in the Elisabethkirche in Pressburg (Bratislava). The animation characteristic of Troger's style is graphically portrayed here in the unbroken pen strokes with agitated, repeated contours. Instead of the usual brush wash for the modelling of light and shade he used natural chalk.

47 GIOVANNI BATTISTA TIEPOLO
(Venice 1696–1770 Madrid)
Reclining youth. Chalk, pen in sepia, wash, 210:158 mm. Albertina, Vienna. Cat. I. 299.

The illusionist style of roof painting presupposes a complete mastery of *sotto in sù* (view from below) perspective. Tiepolo acquired this mastery by making study after study, which give a foretaste of the romantic grandeur of his paintings. With relaxed strokes of the pen, which frequently leave the contours open, he brings out a few essential features, while the brush provides the delicate modelling of body and space.

48 PIETRO DA CORTONA (Cortona 1596–1669 Rome)
Madonna with Child and Saints. Black chalk on grained paper, 320:260 mm. Uffizi, Florence.
Cortona's sketch of a 'Santa Conversazione' for an altar painting combines disciplined composition with baroque sentiment. By using a particularly hard chalk on rough-grained paper he achieves an effect of optical relaxation without having to sacrifice linear precision.

49 GIOVANNI BATTISTA PIAZZETTA (Venice 1682–1754)
Study of a girl's head and hand. Black chalk, 280:284 mm. Albertina, Vienna. Cat. I. 249.
Piazzetta achieves a remarkable effect of actuality by his varied use of graphic media. The white chalk applied with varying emphasis on the tinted paper provides the unusually attractive surface texture, while the white highlights and empty spaces give the picture light and life.

50 JEAN-BAPTISTE ISABEY (Nancy 1767–1855 Paris)
Portrait caricature. Brush in ink, *c.* 1815. 348:207 mm. Kupferstichkabinett, Akademie der bildenden Künste, Vienna.
The subject is probably Prince Clemens Metternich, whom Isabey could have met at the Vienna Congress. Pure brush drawing with diluted ink; the darker parts with undiluted ink.

51 FRANCISCO DE GOYA
(Fuendetodos 1746–1828 Bordeaux)
Procession. Brush in sepia, *c.* 1818. 205:139 mm. Kupferstichkabinett, Stiftung Preussischer Kulturbesitz, Staatliche Museen, Berlin. Reproduction in original size.
Pure brush drawing with strong painterly colour effects. The individual tone values convey space and figures and also colours. The half-tones, ranging from the areas of strongest light, from the whiteness of the original paper, to the very dark, almost black areas, are achieved by various layers of colour applied when the previous layer had dried.

52 EUGÈNE DELACROIX
(Charenton-Saint-Maurice 1798–1863 Paris)
The Rape of Rebecca. Pencil, 1864. 237:207 mm. Louvre, Paris. Cat. gen. 3445. Reproduction slightly reduced. Composition study for a painting in the New York Metropolitan Museum.
The search for form is clearly discernible in the delicate lines around the contours. The final version shows much stronger lines.

53 HONORÉ DAUMIER
(Marseilles 1808–78 Valmondois)
Fairground Crier (La Parade). Black chalk, pen and ink over charcoal and red ochre, 390:307 mm. Museum of Fine Arts, Budapest. Preliminary drawing for three of the five figures in the watercolour *La Parade* in the Louvre.
Daumier manages to express in graphic terms both the emotional and the humorous side of the figures at the fair. The composition of this drawing, which is deliberately based on a series of triangles, is relaxed and animated by means of short, wavy lines. The use of different materials reinforces the impression of transience, whereas the repetition of certain contours introduces plastic values.

54 GEORGES SEURAT (Paris 1859–91)
Café Concert. c. 1887. Black chalk and gouache, 235:205 mm. Museum of Art, Rhode Island School of Design, Providence. Seligmann 58. Reproduction in original size.
Seurat employs the pointillist technique of painting in monochrome drawing and so achieves an atmospheric 'painting' by graphic means.

55 HENRI MATISSE (Le Cateau 1869–1954 Nice)
Seated girl. 1939. Charcoal, 640:500 mm. Galerie Berggruen, Paris.
Into the simple framework of this monumental composition Matisse introduces a decorative check pattern, which, however, by slight changes of direction and underlining certain parts of the body also renders volumes. The smudged charcoal gives added clarity to the background and lends an impression of colour.

56 PAUL KLEE
(Münchenbuchsee, Berne 1879–1940 Muralto-Locarno)
Canal docks. Pen and ink over hard pencil, wash, 1910. 76:249 mm. Albertina, Vienna. Reproduction slightly reduced.
By rapid 'wet-on-wet' work the lines of the pen are made to run. Strangely biomorphic 'growth-buds' shoot up in the 'sultry' atmosphere. The appeal of the casual is deliberately invoked.

57 VINCENT VAN GOGH
(Groot Zundert 1853–90 Auvers-sur-Oise)
Farm in Provence. Reed pen and ink over pencil drawing, 1888. 395:540 mm. Gemeente Museum, Amsterdam. De la Faille 1478.
With the straight lines of a reed pen Van Gogh achieves a very compact, flat and decorative effect.

39

40

41

42

43

44

45

46

47

48

49

mistère queer.

50

51

54

55

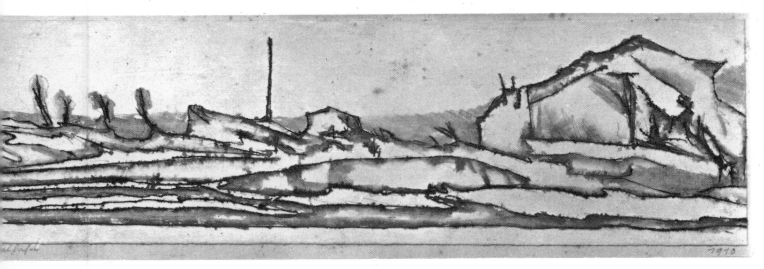

56

57

Techniques of Drawing

The large number of drawing media and the almost unlimited scope both for combining the various techniques and for introducing painting methods make it impossible to break drawing down into clear-cut, technical categories. Moreover, most drawing media are so flexible in themselves that the creative artist is by no means bound to employ a specific technique in order to achieve a specific result. The calligraphic line can, like the broad stroke, be produced in a variety of ways; flat effects are not solely achieved by brushwork. Finally, the pure contrast of light and shade can be considerably modified by a theoretically unlimited number of intermediate tones as well as by a change in colouring. In other words, the choice of technical medium depends both on the artist's ultimate objective and on his personal preference. If in the course of history certain techniques have been preferred in certain periods, this is almost always attributable to the prevalent style rather than to the technical possibilities open to the artist.

Considerably too much emphasis has also been laid on the distinction, which largely decides the nature of line, between direct, self-drawing media (etching needle, graphite, charcoal, chalk), which produce a continuous line dependent only on the pressure of the hand, and indirect, relaying media (pen or brush), which must stop and restart. Furthermore, artists have always been tempted to explore and expand the special qualities of individual media and thereby obscure still further the by no means clearly defined borderline between hard and thin, and between soft and broad.

Direct Media

Hard Points

Hard points with their thin, even lines are essentially linear media. In ancient times metal points had already begun to replace the familiar wax tablet and stylus and they continued in use in the medieval scriptoria until the sixteenth century. Though to a lesser degree, the metal stylus was also employed, particularly to supply perspective for certain constructions and guide-lines for architectural drawings. In the nineteenth century it even experienced a kind of romantic revival. But the most common medium was the relatively soft lead pencil, which could also be used effectively on smooth surfaces. The massive pencils usually had a handle, frequently ornamentally carved, and two points, or they merely had soldered points of the colouring material, as was customary with silverpoint. In addition to lead, tin and copper are also mentioned as writing metals, as well as various alloys of tin and lead and finally silver.

The soft grey, easily erasable stroke of the lead stylus was preferred for practice drawings and preliminary drawings; for the final version the line is not sufficiently distinctive and durable. In many cases only the print-marks of stylus drawings have survived; most were subsequently copied in ink (*Ills. 19, 35, 38*).

Silverpoint is better suited to careful studies and drawings. By contrast with other metal points, the ground, whether parchment or paper, must be specially prepared for a silverpoint drawing. This ensures that the line, once drawn, does not fade and cannot be erased. The delicate stroke, which is originally a soft grey but quickly oxidizes to a brownish colour, requires a very precise concept of form and a sure hand. If silverpoint is used for sketching or in the search for form, the individual phases of the drawing remain visible (*Ill. 1*; Plate V). In completed drawings plastic qualities and contrasts of light and shade can only be achieved within the limited scope of the slender line, by parallel or cross hatching and by linear repetition. Despite the fact that the silverpoint drawing calls for careful preparation and a steady hand, it has remained a favourite medium for travel sketches.

Whereas other metal points were almost completely replaced by more recent media such as charcoal, chalk and graphite – which is frequently referred to in old reports as 'lead pencil' – silverpoint has remained in use to this day, at least as an outsider.

Towards the end of the sixteenth century sticks of graphite, fitted in holders, seem to have emerged in England and Spain quite independently as implements for writing and sketching and to have become quickly popular. The graphite pencils which were originally used in their natural state – relatively soft, smudgy and containing fragments of stone – were used largely for preliminary drawings, which had to be copied in a more durable material. Like charcoal, they were also used for transferring cartoons and for tracing. Today, however, relatively few traces are left and those that survive can hardly be distinguished from soft metal-point drawings. Graphite, seen in indirect light, also has a metallic shimmer, which explains why for a long time it was regarded as a metal. Although graphite was in common use throughout Europe for writing and for less important drawings, it was seldom used for artists' drawings. Only in Holland was it used for other than preliminary drawings. J. B. Weenix and quite a few portrait artists worked with 'Spanish lead', and Albert Cuyp made artistic use of it in the landscape drawing, when he employed the lighter graphite for his background and the more colourful chalk for the foreground. Graphite was more often used to produce flat tones, the lighter parts being rubbed out and the dark areas reinforced or even done with another material.

The graphite pencil only gained full recognition as a drawing medium in its own right with Nicolas-Jacques Conté's invention around 1790. By an appropriate mixture of clay and graphite any degree of hardness could be achieved, producing a clear, durable line. Within a short time this 'lead pencil' was being used both for sketches and for independent drawings in preference to all other pencils, and it was ideally suited to the clear linear style of the classicists with their careful modelling of volumes. Ingres was one of the first outstanding artists to use the lead pencil. By combining a delicate linearity of form with a carefully accentuated line structure, he achieves both plastic values and at the same time an uncommonly strong yet sensitive surface appeal (Ill. p. 35).

The specially hardened graphite pencil, which in technique and effect is very like the silverpoint, is the favourite material of the romantics, Nazarenes and Pre-Raphaelites. The potentialities of the hard pencil for producing precise linear contours have been exploited above all by illustrators, from the early nineteenth century (Flaxman, Richter, Schwind, Rossetti, Führich) to Art Nouveau (Beardsley) and to the present time (Steinberg, Flora). The German neoclassicists (the Olivier brothers) and C. D. Friedrich, like Corot in France, also achieved a relaxed, intimate atmosphere and the most delicate modelling with the hard pencil.

Softer pencils are preferred by artists with an interest in painting, whose drawings are sketches and rough drawings rather than finished works (Delacroix, *Ill. 52*). Menzel favoured broad carpenters' pencils, using the narrow side for contours and the broad side for deep shadows and flat hatchings *(Ill. 8)*. Winslow Homer exploits all the possibilities to the full in his realistic, often atmospherically heightened, pictorial compositions *(Ill. 7)*. Cézanne developed a style of his own, distinguishing one object from the next by means of parallel hatchings running in different directions, thus avoiding pure line and translating the solidity of objects into graphic, two-dimensional terms (Plate IX). Rodin achieved a plastic effect when he blurred the contours with a wet finger, thus producing a diminishing flat tone which is at its lightest in the foreground, at it thickest in the more remote parts. A similar effect was produced by A. Giacometti, who gently rubbed over the pencil lines with an eraser *(Ill. 36)*. In Gustav Klimt's pencil drawings contour and detail are inextricably linked *(Ill. 9)*.

Since the end of the nineteenth century coloured pencils, in which dyes are mixed with the graphite and clay or even replace the graphite, have been used to add colour to pencil drawings. For artists' drawings their use is limited by comparison with coloured crayons. Klimt sometimes has recourse to coloured pencils to introduce reds or blues into his drawings. Picasso uses not only simple coloured pencils but also a multicoloured pencil, which contains all the various leads together, so that with a mere turn of the hand he can switch from one colour to another (Plate XIV).

Soft points

Charcoal as a cheap, readily available medium for drawing must surely have been in use before Greek antiquity, when the first literary records of it appeared. In all painters' manuals much space is devoted to the choice of wood and to the length of the carbonizing process required to produce a charcoal that will colour easily, is not too brittle and is reasonably durable. Charcoal was the ideal material for preparatory drawings of all kinds, directly on the wall or panel, but also – because of the ease with which it could be handled or corrected – for sketches and for formal designs to be developed later. The possibility of drawing fine lines with the sharpened edge and at the same time quickly producing with the broad edge contours which were large and easily visible was a guarantee of its success. Particularly in cartoons, charcoal has become indispensable both for drawing and for transferring contours through the pricked paper to the painting surface *(Ill. 18)*. Charcoal has also played an important part both in the training of artists and in the formal evolution of the individual work. Traces of charcoal preliminary drawings can be found under many pen and brush drawings, and also in chalk drawings, pastels and watercolours, not to mention the charcoal contours in pictures.

Charcoal became accepted as a medium for independent drawings or works, which had to be preserved for some time, only when an appropriate method had been found to fix the powdery, easily smudged line. Many of the older charcoal drawings which have survived were fixed later, as is apparent from the traces of smudging, often all too serious, and from the damage done by rubbing; but by the beginning of the sixteenth century at the latest artists were fixing their own works.

Pure charcoal drawings as independent works are rare, apart from the portrait study. In Holland charcoal was frequently supplemented by pen and chalk in order to achieve plastic values and to exploit the difference in tone between the faint, light grey charcoal line and the deep black, close-grained chalk. A fairly large number of pure charcoal drawings by the Dutch animal painter Paulus Potter (1625–54) are still extant. Drawing with charcoal became more widespread again in the nineteenth century, which prized the relaxed line and the sketch for their own sake. By means of slight smudging and shading, it could also introduce painterly qualities into drawing. Degas in particular, who favoured any kind of soft point, used charcoal for many sketch-like drawings. In the twentieth century Ernst Barlach and Käthe Kollwitz have worked mainly with charcoal. Henri Matisse has also used this medium to the full to give a painterly quality to a monumental composition by the contrast of hard lines and soft shading *(Ill. 55)*.

Greater durability and a deeper, richer, black line can be achieved with oiled charcoal. However, once the charcoal has been soaked in linseed oil it no longer rubs out easily and therefore requires a sure and steady hand. Its use was confined to the sixteenth and seventeenth centuries. Tintoretto and the Bolognese academicians employed it; then, in the seventeenth century, it was much more widely used in Holland. Almost all the artists of the Rubens school worked with the broader, vigorous, deep black oil charcoal, which frequently sheds its excess fat in the margin *(Ill. 17)* and soaks through the paper. The brownish colour gives a warm patina to many of these drawings. With the emergence of the pastel crayon, oil charcoal disappeared almost entirely.

Like the graphite and 'lead' pencil, stone or natural chalk holds an intermediate position in relation to the hard-drawing points. In its natural state black chalk is clay with a carbon content in a great variety of admixtures which decide the degree of purity and hardness. In addition to the natural chalk described by Meder as producing a 'greybrown or grey-black matt line, beneath which scratches caused by sandy ingredients are often clearly visible', soft and deep black chalks were also used. The chalks from Piedmont and Spain were particularly sought after, but deposits are known to have been found throughout Europe. Undoubtedly these natural chalks were also broken down, cleansed and compressed into sticks, which in their purity and smoothness are not unlike artificial chalks.

As against the minute and fine detail produced by a hard point, chalk drawing provides and indeed requires a much freer, more sweeping line. In the history of artists' drawings the transition, towards the end of the fifteenth century, from the delicate lines of the metal point to the broad, relatively hard lines of natural chalk and to the even softer lines of artificial chalk marks an important turning point.

Leonardo, who is generally credited with the invention of artificial chalk, used it both in preliminary drawings and for producing tone, frequently in conjunction with other techniques (for example with tints of various colours, *Ill. 29*). The draughtsmen from central Italy realized and exploited to the full the potentialities of chalk as a means of subduing and softening sharp contours without sacrificing firm, plastic form. Raphael and his pupils, such as Guilio Romano, and the Florentines who were influenced by him (Fra Bartolommeo, Andrea del Sarto) employed this gritty yet pliant material, which, by smudging, can also produce flat tonal effects. Michelangelo also used chalk for architectural drawings. In his free-flowing line, which summarizes so much detail, Pontormo exploited the granular composition of the chalk to lend animation to his stroke (Ill. 24). Cortona's monumentally designed and carefully composed group of figures (Ill. 48) conveys an optical impression of relaxation by a frequent and uncoordinated interruption of the exact line drawn in hard chalk on coarse-grained paper in order to highlight plastic values. The northern Italians, and especially the Venetians from Titian to Piazzetta, achieved striking painterly effects with chalk, which permits a delicate differentiation of light and shade.

In the north it was Dürer once again who exploited all the potentialities of the material and used chalk with graphic finesse and yet in monumental form; in his later period he used chalk by preference for portrait drawings. While Dürer's immediate successors tended to preserve the clear, precise line, Grünewald adopted the broad line and painterly, smudging method of chalk drawing.

Pieter Bruegel the Elder achieved an overall effect which is compact and painterly in his detailed but by no means crowded nature studies (Ill. 2). The lively strokes in Rubens' and Van Dyck's chalk drawings (Ill. 5) swell and recede to give an effect of vigour and majesty. Rembrandt often employed natural chalk for studies in nature; in his elephants, for example (Ill. p. 133), the granular character of the medium enabled him to reproduce the texture of the animal's hide. The landscape and marine painters (J. van Goyen, E. van de Velde) frequently combined natural chalk with graphite or even charcoal.

Since the seventeenth century natural chalk has given way more and more to artificial chalk, which, by virtue of its deeper tone, its smoother consistency which facilitates a uniform line, and its varying degrees of hardness, was a particularly appropriate medium for the baroque draughtsman with his preference for painterly refinement and modulation. The artificial chalks are produced from soot, primarily lamp-black; they can be made in many degrees of hardness down to a soft, sticky mass.

The chalk drawing attained a position of great importance in the eighteenth and nineteenth centuries. In the art schools then to be found all over Europe, artificial chalk was the most widely used medium for all kinds of studies; it was just as widely used for independent drawings, in particular portrait drawings. Preparatory drawings for other technical purposes were also done for the most part in chalk, because it is unlikely to smudge,

can be applied with greater precision and reacts more immediately to pressure of the hand than charcoal or graphite. Furthermore it adapts itself ideally to all styles. Piazzetta, for example, in his studies (Ill. 49) exploited in the most delicate way the painterly potentialities of soft chalk, from deep blacks to lightly smudged hatching, and its wide range of line and tone. A good example of plastic modelling combined with precise execution in a chalk preliminary drawing is David's study of a seated woman (Ill. 16), which was squared for transfer to canvas.

Seurat opened up entirely new possibilities for the use of chalk when, by applying the form-dissecting method of the pointillists and translating it into monochrome terms, he achieved a flat tonal effect. The grandiose effect of the broad, deep black line and its spontaneous, calligraphic character is to be found in the work of almost all twentieth-century artists, both in abstract and in graphic compositions. The expressionists in particular made frequent use of chalk in their portrait studies, and by an economical use of line they achieved a high degree of intensity (Beckmann, Kokoschka).

By comparison with the black natural chalk, the brown variants play a subordinate role, as they are used almost exclusively to provide colour effects. The brown tone can be due to deterioration, unless soft brown charcoal or manganese dioxide (a by-product of red chalk) has been added. But much more important as a drawing medium on its own merits is an iron-oxide form of chalk: red chalk.

Although it is one of the oldest known drawing media, the earliest evidence of its artistic use is around 1500. Leonardo appears to have been the first to use red chalk not only for rough sketches but also on its own (drawings for the equestrian statue of Francesco Sforza and for *The Last Supper*). Red chalk introduced a new element into drawing: colour. This painterly component is further enhanced by the generally much greater softness of red chalk, which reduces the contrast with the paper. Compared with black chalk, red chalk drawings have soft shadows and a matt shimmer. This unique combination of line drawing and colour values made red chalk a favourite medium of the mannerists. The rigorous plastic values and moving grandeur of Michelangelo's *Head of a woman* (Plate X) are softened by the medium without losing anything of the monumental effect. Whereas

REMBRANDT HARMENSZ. VAN RIJN (Leiden 1606–69 Amsterdam)
Elephant. Chalk, 1637. 233:355 mm. Albertina, Vienna. Benesch 457.
With loosely drawn lines Rembrandt captures the qualities of the animal's hide and movement.
This study from nature, signed and dated as an independent drawing, was used again in the
etching *Adam and Eve* of 1638

Raphael used red chalk for preliminary drawings (Plate III) and seldom used it for a complete drawing, Fra Bartolommeo and Andrea del Sarto drew equally if not more often in red as in black chalk. Correggio's drawings are, for the most part, in the painterly, soft, colourful red chalk. The same material, varying from bright red to brown, was also very popular in France (Martin Fréminet, François Clouet).

Quite apart from its colour property, red chalk has several other, distinctly painterly qualities: the various nuances of colour, the ease with which it can be rubbed to produce fine shading or flat-tone smudging, and finally the varying thickness with which the colour can be applied. With moistened chalk it may be very compact, or with a very light stroke it may be extremely relaxed. Thanks to its unusually wide range of potentialities, red chalk became a favourite medium for styles and artists with a penchant for colour. Jacob Jordans produced pure red chalk drawings. Rembrandt and his circle, on the other hand, only used red chalk in exceptional cases.

Red chalk achieved its widest popularity and use as a drawing material in eighteenth-century France. Watteau exploited all the tonal and painterly potentialities of the various colour nuances of red chalk and its combination with black chalks. The predominantly warm-toned colour was bound to make a special appeal to such a sensual century. In addition to studies, figure compositions and portrait drawings, landscape drawings were also produced in this technique (Hubert Robert). Very often red chalk was employed in preliminary drawings for reproduction of engraving, as it is particularly easy to transfer by means of pressure on damp paper. This reverse impression could serve as a direct pattern for printing. In the course of

133

the nineteenth century, red chalk was used less and less as a drawing medium on its own. However, because of its warm tone and its soft surface appeal, it was still widely used to portray the female body (Bonnard, Maillol).

White chalk (calcium carbonate), which is also a natural mineral, and steatite play a minor role as independent drawing media in preliminary drawings and sketches on a coloured ground, but they are widely used in combination with other colours to provide white highlights both in the dry state and when melted down and applied with the brush.

Depending on the number involved, a combination of chalks of various colours is known as 'à deux crayons', usually meaning black chalk for drapery and hair and red chalk for flesh tones on white paper, or 'à trois crayons', when the additional tone is achieved by using white chalk or coloured paper or both. This expressly colouristic method, which brings drawing very close to painting, was practised as early as the fifteenth century and is also found in silverpoint and pen drawings (cf. Master ES, Ill. 39). It was still more widely used in the chalk drawings of the sixteenth century. Hans Holbein the Younger, in particular, built up his portrait studies in colour and added to the black and red tones other coloured chalks as well as touches with pen and brush (Plate VI). Equally colourful are the portrait heads of Jean, and even more of François Clouet in France. Rubens not only draws portraits with two or three chalks (Plate VIII); he also uses the various colours to liven up his landscape drawings. Watteau achieved a harmony which had been unknown until then in his drawings with two or three chalks of different colours. The differentiation of tone, the care he takes with his texture and the great sensual appeal of his delicate drawings (Plate XV) had a decisive influence on the style of drawing of the entire eighteenth century (Ill. 25).

Further scope for the use of colour in drawing is provided by the pastel crayons, produced from mineral as well as plant dyes mixed with white clay and various binding agents. The great wealth of colour which was opened up by the pastel drawing was fully exploited only in the eighteenth century, although coloured crayons are known to have been produced and used since the sixteenth century in Italy and also in France and Germany. The portrait studies of Hans Holbein the Younger (Plate VI), which are primarily works of draughtsmanship, are quite different artistically from pastel paintings, like those of Rosalba Carriera (Plate XII). Her pastels with the delicate colours applied with a dry stumper are closer to painting than any other dry medium has ever come. The great popularity and widespread use made of this technique did not entirely disappear during the classical period, but it was not until the late nineteenth century that coloured chalks became more frequently used for the more pictorial type of drawing. Edgar Degas employed this technique in order to capture the special appeal of the dancers and the atmosphere of the stage in artificial light (Plate XIII). Odilon Redon's floral still-life pictures owe their aesthetic charm to the heavy application of glowing pastel colours. Later in the twentieth century pastel crayons were used for the distinct purpose of emphasizing tonal line (E. Munch, E. L. Kirchner).

Indirect Media

Pen

Regardless of changing styles, the pen, thanks to its capacity to respond to the most varied artistic

demands, has remained the most consistently popular drawing medium. Although the principle of the pen has remained the same for thousands of years, the actual material used has undergone frequent changes. A pointed, bent nib picks up the colouring liquid and, by virtue of the capillary effect of the split point, sheds it again more or less evenly, depending on the pressure applied and on the degree of saturation. Pens for writing or drawing, which in ancient times were made from reeds, have always found favour with individual draughtsmen who preferred a firm, rather hard line. But the more pliable, softer quill pen remained the most popular instrument for drawing from the early Middle Ages until the nineteenth century. The wing-feathers of geese, and also of swans and ravens, are particularly recommended in artists' manuals. Since the middle of the nineteenth century the metal pen has gained the ascendancy, as it can be produced in various degrees of hardness and elasticity, so that the choice of pen in itself presupposes certain formal limitations.

The artistic scope of the pen drawing ranges from the thin, even, contour drawing to the broad, flat line and all forms of stippling and hatching. It embraces all the functions of drawing, from the first rough sketch to the completed, independent work. In no other form of drawing is the personal 'signature' of the draughtsman so clearly displayed, regardless of contemporary style, as in the pen drawing.

The late Middle Ages and the early Renaissance preferred the thin line of the outline drawing with closed contours and virtually no plastic modelling (*Ills 10, 11, 28*; Ill. p. 9). Where the artist wanted to introduce plastic and painterly elements into the linear graphic system of the pen drawing, he did so by a series of short lines and schematic hatching, by interrupting his contours and by varying the quality of the loosely overlapping lines (*Ills 10, 13, 19, 39*). In Dürer's pen drawings one can follow the transition from the purely graphic to the plastic pen drawing at the same time as the growth in refinement between his early work and his later years (Plate IV).

The differences in methods of drawing emerge more clearly in the sixteenth century than at any subsequent period. Each of the 'classicists' of the Renaissance found in the pen the formal potentialities which corresponded to his particular style.

Leonardo's scientific drawings–anatomical, mechanical and geological (*Ill. 29*)–are almost unrivalled in their precision. Raphael's pen drawings, which are mostly sketches and studies, express the artist's intentions in a few, relaxed strokes and uninhibited alterations of form (Plate III). By means of apposite cross-hatching, Michelangelo brings out the volume of his figures. Baccio Bandinelli reinforced his style of drawing with deliberately vigorous lines (*Ill. 30*). Titian modelled his figures with short, curved, parallel lines and creates effects of light and shade by leaving empty spaces and by drawing broad hatches over the picture (*Ill. 32*). The tiny loops and scrolls which Altdorfer used to depict foliage, folds in drapery, skin and hair give a surface quality that is exciting and vibrant (*Ill. 40*). Within the sweeping lines of his main contours Hans Baldung Grien introduced precise parallel and cross-hatchings side by side with bizarre, ornamentalized forms, which hold their own in the overall design (Plate XI). Jan Swart van Groningen used thin, mobile lines to merge the contours of figures and objects into larger complexes, in which modelling is merely suggested (*Ill. 41*). A similar technique was adopted by Bartholomäus Spranger (*Ill. 23*) towards the end of the sixteenth century, while Pieter Bruegel the Elder modelled with layers of lines and produced differences of tone by using various tints (*Ill. 2*). Characteristic of the central Italian mannerists is plastic modelling by means of short parallel hatching and curving swelling strokes which fade out, thin and sharp, into the flat (*Ill. 21*). The Venetian draughtsmen, on the other hand, expressed plastic properties by means of a linear technique which, by contrast with the firmness of the contours, is so relaxed as to appear almost capricious (*Ill. 12*). The technique of thickening the lines at the joints, which is typical of a modelling style of drawing, was deliberately reversed by the northern Italian Luca Cambiaso in his cubist figures: the clearly-drawn lines break off at the joints, thus creating an impression of abstract movement (*Ill. 15*). The element of mobility in Jacques Callot's small-scale studies derives from the uninhibited use of the pen, which embraces both body and pose with ornamental verve. The painterly trend of the seventeenth century, combined with a basically mannerist approach, emerges clearly here in the contrasts of light and shade which transcend all detail (*Ill. 26*).

SAUL STEINBERG (Ramnicul, Rumania 1914)
The Painter in his Studio. Pen, 300:220 mm. From *Passport*.
The ironical contrast between the ornamentally overfurnished studio and the puritanical con-
structivist picture is graphically echoed in the 'open' style of the drawing, and the omission of
contour lines round the painter

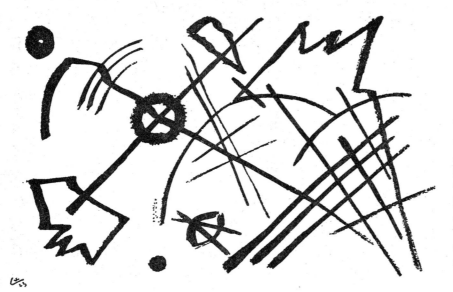

WASSILY KANDINSKY
(Moscow 1866–1944 Neuilly-sur-Seine)
Drawing 8, 1923.
Point, line and plane are ingredients
which Kandinsky employs as consistently
in his drawings as he champions non-
objective art in his theoretical writings.
The 'theme' is a concentration on the
tension and balance of these basic elements of drawing

In the seventeenth century the pure pen drawing
was superseded by the introduction of brush wash
as a complement to the pen. The broad line itself
produces effects of light, and closed contours give
way to a vibrant, open style of drawing. Line was
no longer employed to describe and circumscribe
the subject matter but actually as a means of expression. This new function of the pen drawing is
clearly illustrated in Rembrandt's works. He
preferred the rougher, broader, more vigorous reed
pen *(Ill. 45)* and combined it with quill pen and
brush; furthermore he stumped damp or dry and
achieved his light effects by leaving blank spaces
or by creating them. In the eighteenth century too
the pen provided the skeleton for the drawing,
which continued to show marked painterly trends.
Tiepolo achieved his main stresses with a pen that
in places is purely calligraphic *(Ill. 47)*. With powerful, wide-sweeping strokes of the pen, supported
by the brush and, by way of contrast, thin, nervous,
jerky lines, Piranesi wove his uncanny architecture
into a dense, graphic pattern *(Ill. 28)*. Around the
middle of the eighteenth century Paul Troger
(Ill. 46) with his thin, clear lines gives us a foretaste
of the classical contour drawing, which reached
its extreme form with John Flaxman (Ill. p. 82)
and Bonaventura Genelli. The romantics reverted
deliberately to the plastic modelling style of the
early Renaissance with studiously drawn hair and
shadows, precise hatching and closed contours.

The German neoclassicists (Koch; Overbeck, Ill.
p. 107; Richter, Plate XVI) are more relaxed but still
lay great emphasis on the thin pen stroke. Again
the predominantly linear style of drawing produced
a more painterly reaction (Delacroix).

In the late nineteenth century all the possible
varieties of pen drawing are represented simultaneously. Daumier employed the pen as one of several
media particularly to bring out characteristic
features *(Ill. 53)*. The clear contour drawing was
revived by Beardsley (Ill. p. 81). Monet's vibrant
lines reflect the pulsating atmosphere; Pissarro
used the pen like a stipple-graver, abandoning line
altogether. Vincent van Gogh, on the other hand,
employed the vigorous line of the reed pen to
create an atmosphere of remarkable tension *(Ill. 57)*.

The great importance attached to the process of
drawing in modern art also opens up promising
new avenues to linear pen drawing. Particularly
characteristic of drawings by artists from Latin
countries (Matisse, Picasso, Modigliani) is a deliberate stripping down to the simple contrast between
the dark line and the flat white space around it
without any plastic illusionism. Kokoschka, Kirchner and Beckmann drew with the reed pen, which
gives a broader, more vigorous line and is in
consequence much more expressive. Alfred Kubin
developed an intricate network of lines, while
Paul Klee's precious linear pattern and pictorial
wit inspired a large number of illustrators (Stein-

berg, Flora). Autonomy of line is often postulated in Kandinsky's two-dimensional drawings (Ill. p. 138), and it reached its climax in the hair-fine, automatic linear compositions of WOLS (Wolfgang Schulze), in which the slightest movement of the artist's hand is reflected.

Brush

The brush drawing represents a transition to painting, both in its technique and in its artistic effect. The history of the brush goes even farther back than that of the pen, which is dependent on papyrus, parchment or paper, whereas the large-scale wall drawings from the ice age onwards were made with the brush. In small format, miniature painting, often very close to the pen drawing, is flat brush-work, so although the brush as an individual medium had been in use for thousands of years, the early brush drawings were produced by the same method as the contemporary pen drawings. They were drawn with a pointed hair brush and – particularly characteristic of brush 'drawing' – within a limited tone-scale, which included monochrome tone values and in addition black and white as contrasting colours, the basic pattern of the first brush drawings in the fifteenth century (Plate V).

The Venetians, starting with Cima da Conegliano, showed remarkable skill in exploiting the possibility of fine nuances and subdued atmosphere. Dürer, who became familiar with this technique during his journey to Venice, used it to devise a system of extremely fine brushstrokes, which can only be distinguished from a pen drawing by the varying strength and length of the strokes. German and Dutch artists worked in a similar fashion in their chiaroscuro drawings (Altdorfer, Baldung). But the Italians, for example Carpaccio, preferred a broader line and filled the smaller areas with homogeneous brushstrokes. Parmigianino went still further with his punctuated, speckling technique, which he employed in drawings, with the flat, chiaroscuro woodcut in mind (Ill. 20). Palma Giovane achieved a particularly painterly form of brush drawing merely by shading areas of tone in such a way that the ground, which is left white, appears as bright light; other parts were gone over with the brush several times to form deep shadows.

In the seventeenth century a combination of brush and pen was also widely used. For the landscape painter the brush drawing is an ideal means of depicting space and light. Claude Lorrain produced the finest nuances of light and shade by varying the wetness of his brush (Ill. 43). Asselijn brings out the plastic values of his figures (Ill. 3) and Salvator Rosa combined a romantic atmosphere with a dramatic use of light (Ill. 6). The artists

GEORGE ROMNEY (Beckside 1734–1802 Kendal)
Lady Hamilton as Ariadne. Brush in bistre, 432:238 mm. Art Institute, Chicago.
This free-flowing brush drawing achieves a monumental and distinctly statuesque effect

139

of the Rubens school (Van Dyck, Jacob Jordans) preserved the graphic, linear qualities even in pure brush drawings. In Holland, Rembrandt in particular exploited the painterly potentialities of brush drawing with unparalleled success (*cf.* Plate II). Adriaen van Ostade and Adriaen Brouwer gave many of their genre scenes the pictorial character of a monochrome watercolour.

The eighteenth century was mainly interested in colour, and the tonality of the monochrome brush drawing did not, therefore, play a leading role. Nevertheless it produced one of the outstanding masters of this technique: Honoré Fragonard. In his landscapes, figure compositions and portraits, accentuated contours, soft chalky lines, a delicate use of tone and deep shadows merge to form pictorially complete compositions *(Ill. 27)*. More dramatic in their contrast of light and shade, which is reminiscent of Rembrandt, are Goya's brush drawings *(Ill. 51)*, in which the clear white of the paper can assume just as much objective importance as the broad lines and flat colours. George Romney's studies are imposing (Ill. p. 139). A caricature portrait by Isabey is a particularly good example of the technique of using ink in various degrees of thickness and applying it in layers to achieve an effect of plastic shading *(Ill. 50)*. The English landscape artists (Constable, Turner) employed the brush to create atmospheric effects in their drawings. With the growing popularity of the multicoloured watercolour in the nineteenth century, the monochrome brush drawing suffered a sharp decline. Yet Géricault, Delacroix and Constantin Guys preserved the authentic character of the brush drawing.

For the twentieth-century artist, the brush as a drawing medium, especially with deep black ink, has become an effective means of two-dimensional composition (Picasso, Kirchner).

Modern Techniques

A number of modern writing and drawing media, such as fountain pens, ball-point pens and felt pens, are comparable in their use to the direct media, but still belong substantially in the category of indirect media. In terms of line, fountain pens are almost indistinguishable from other metal points. They respond to manual pressure, giving an increased flow of ink and thick line under strong pressure, a thin, even line when pressure is relaxed.

Only where complete uniformity even of long lines has been achieved can one be sure that a fountain pen has been used.

Ball-point pens, on the other hand, always produce an even line and are incapable of modulation. Characteristics are the round tip and the 'omission' of the continuous line resulting from the fact that the ball-point passes so lightly over the paper. This pen has not acquired any artistic significance.

The felt pen also gives an indifferent performance, its capacity to transmit colour depending on the absorbency of the textile point. This medium, which is more suitable for technical purposes and is seldom used artistically (Heinz Troekes), produces an apparently strong, unmodulated line, which can be applied uniformly in the flat, producing, for the most part, a vigorous tone effect.

Grease crayons give a particularly soft, thick line and are also applicable to very smooth surfaces such as glass and porcelain. This medium, originally developed for technical purposes, soon became widely used and was produced in many colours.

Composite Techniques

In no other branch of art does the combination of various techniques play such a major artistic role as in drawing. As in painting, so too in drawing it is possible to distinguish a rough drawing, which is done in a medium that can be easily corrected and which is materially overlaid by the finished work, from the finished work itself (*cf. Ills 1, 2, 18, 19, 20, 27, 28, 34, 38, 44*; Plates I, V). As against this difference in treatment of rough drawing and finished drawing, the employment of various techniques to supplement each other within one and the same drawing is a conscious stylistic device. By far the most popular combination is that of pen and brush.

The use of flat colour to fill out the contours of closed-line drawings goes back to the tradition of book illustration. Colouring is not dependent on the sketching artist's hand, and has often been added later. More significant from an artistic viewpoint is the use of wash, usually in a dilute form of the same medium as the drawing itself. Individual objects or parts of the picture are uniformly toned within or along the contours. By applying several coats to the same part, fine differentiations and imperceptible transitions to stronger tones can be achieved. For deep shadows a more concentrated colour is employed, a good example being Cambiaso's cubist figures (Ill. 15). A wash is frequently used for modelling, especially in the sixteenth century, and it continued to be used as a means of lending spatial and plastic shape to drawing. Delicate brushstrokes, running outwards from the lines of the pen drawing into the flat, create individual effects of shade in figures and folds of drapery and enhance the plastic values (Ills 23, 47). In addition to extensive flat wash and shade modelling, a further differential element is introduced by using the brush for treatment of detail in the same tone as the wash; J. Swart's sketch for a glass window shows how all three methods can be used (Ill. 41).

A further elaboration of the wash technique is achieved by using several colours and tones. The Venetians in particular ran the whole gamut of light and shade (Paolo Veronese), while the Dutch landscape painters of the sixteenth century introduced blue as a third colour in order to emphasize the colour effect (P. Bruegel the Elder, H. Bol, P. Bril). As a means of objective definition this technique remained in use throughout the seventeenth century and was taken up again in the nineteenth (Plate XVI). The accentuation with the brush of individual parts which are essential to the composition, in order to highlight the main figures or define a situation in space has also been a recurrent feature of drawing, ever since the early preparatory drawings (Ills 14, 53).

In the seventeenth century the fruitful relationship between pen and brush received its widest application. The structure of the pen drawing was expanded and enriched; by the use of the brush, open contours were given cohesion (Ill. 42) or, on the other hand, the pen was used to introduce striking features into a composition carried out predominantly with the brush (Ill. 43). The closest association of pen and brush is found in the drawings of Rembrandt (Ill. 45; Plate II). The broad, temperamental pen strokes combine to form dense, flat areas, while the shading produces a markedly plastic and spatial effect; the whole composition is heightened into a study of light by brilliant contrasts in a way that is almost unparalleled in all the techniques of drawing. This apparently quite arbitrary, subjective, vigorous style of drawing, which also manages to portray the most delicate detail with great feeling, became known as the 'Rembrandt method' and had many imitators, none of whom succeeded in rivalling the master.

Compared with the combination of pen and brush, other wash methods remained relatively unimportant. The Dutch nature studies of the seventeenth century are frequently chalk drawings with ink wash (Van Goyen and again Rembrandt). To achieve a markedly grey wash, diluted ink or charcoal dust dissolved in water were used. Washes with a solution of red chalk were employed in portrait drawings and also to give tone to a whole work. Another popular method was the application of red chalk with a wet brush to give the drawing warmth.

When plastic modelling is achieved with dark ink or colour, light reflections can be emphasized by the use of white highlighting, which has the effect of projecting convex bodies from the flat. The use of a white body colour to bring out areas of light is a method borrowed from painting and has been in constant use since antiquity in monumental painting and book illustration. In keeping with the style of the period, white highlights were employed in the sixteenth century (Ills 21, 40) and again in classicism (Ill. 6) for plastic modelling. In chiaroscuro drawing on tinted paper they can take over the modelling of the whole or part of the picture (Plate XI). The seventeenth and eighteenth centuries with their strong leaning towards painting, used white for light effects, as optical phenomena, without defining their source (Ill. 17; Plate VIII). In addition to white-lead, which often oxidizes and turns brown (cf. Plate II), heightening with white chalk was also customary in crayon or chalk drawings, particularly in the 'à deux crayons' or 'à trois crayons' works (Ill. 25; Plate XV).

This relatively limited range of colour can be extended by the wide variety of watercolours. The delicate toning with various colours, which is a feature, for example, of Dürer's *Madonna with the many animals* (Plate IV), is not allowed to overshadow the pen drawing, which continues to dominate, so that this method holds the balance between solid blocks of colour and the wash with its limited range. It was not until the end of the eighteenth century that watercolours really came into their own. The English landscape artists in particular (Alexander and John Cozens, Thomas Gainsborough), exploited the wide colour potentialities of the various media – pen, brush, chalk.

By combining these with various washes and water-colours, they achieved delicate atmospheric effects in their landscape drawings, which reach their climax in Turner's work (Plate VII). Cézanne, on the other hand, used watercolour in his fine pencil drawings in order to translate the volume of objects into a coloured graphic equivalent. At the same time, the introduction of watercolours into drawing and the subordination of the linear element, meant a transition to a new technique with an artistic identity of its own, the watercolour.

Drawing Inks

By far the most popular drawing medium for both pen and brush is writing-ink, which was in common use by early draughtsmen in the medieval scriptoria and has remained in use ever since. For hundreds of years its basic ingredients were oak-gall and iron-oxide, until the nineteenth century when oak-gall was replaced by chemical substances. This so-called iron-gall ink runs black with distinct traces of violet-grey or purple-grey. In the course of time, however, oxidization turns it brown, so that many drawings which today are brown (cf. Plate I) have in fact lost their original colour. By comparison with other brown drawing materials, ink has a distinctive, dark shade and an opaqueness where it has been thickly applied and has come out darker than in the simple line. But the surest way to recognize it is to look at the back of the drawing, for the high acid content of the iron vitriol eats through the paper in course of time.

In the manual by Theophilus, to which we have already referred, the process of manufacturing ink is described: bark of the thorn tree must be thoroughly lixiviated in water, the resultant brew thickened and finally boiled in wine. For stocking and transporting, the ink is then dried into lumps or sticks and, before being used, must again be boiled, preferably in wine.

Certain other inks have a basic carbon content without iron, so that they do not undergo any change. The deep black Indian ink is made from the soot of burnt hardwoods (olive or vine) or from fatty lamp-black, to which gum arabic is usually added as a fixative. This strong black, thick ink, which is light grey when diluted, is produced in solid form, in sticks, especially in the seventeenth century, and dipped in water before being used. The descriptive word 'Indian', or sometimes 'Chinese', indicates its origin: in ancient Egypt, India and China, this particular kind of ink was the most common medium used by painters and writers for thousands of years. It was also produced in Europe from the same ingredients as early as the fifteenth century and was particularly popular among the Dutch and German draughtsmen of the fifteenth and sixteenth centuries. (Ill. 39; Plates IV, XI), especially in chiaroscuro drawings, to contrast sharply with the tinted paper (Ill. 40). The eighteenth-century Italians (Canaletto, Guardi) used diluted ink to introduce shadows into their bistre drawings. In the nineteenth century black Indian ink took precedence over all other writing materials.

Bistre is another by-product of rust and is derived from the fatty deposit on chimney walls. As distinct from Indian ink, it is always brown; the nuances vary according to the kind of wood burnt; oak, for example, produces a particularly dark tone. Bistre, which so far as we know, was not used as writing ink, gives a mild, transparent colour and has a fluid quality, which produces a smooth, even line and also makes it particularly suitable for wash and for the tonal treatment of large areas. After

XVI Ludwig Richter (Dresden 1803–84)
Landscape near Serpentara. Pen and brush in sepia and bistre, blue watercolour, 1825. 285:220 mm. Kupferstichkabinett, Akademie der bildenden Künste, Vienna.
Varied application of (yellowish-brown) bistre and (violet-brown) sepia for the shaded trees on the right and clump of stones and bushes in the left foreground. In his use of blue watercolour Richter reverted to the mannerist three-colour technique of the sixteenth century

being constantly used from the fourteenth century onwards (Plates II, III, XVI), towards the end of the eighteenth century it was replaced by the more intense sepia.

Sepia is the only drawing material with animal origins: it is produced from the dark brown-black pigment of the cuttlefish. According to Pliny and other sources, it was widely used in the ancient world, but there is no concrete evidence of its use before the eighteenth century. As distinct from the brown tone of bistre, sepia gives a darker nuance and a cooler quality, with similar tonal effects as the brown ochres (cf. Plate XVI). To bring out the tonal nuances, sepia is frequently mixed with other dyes. In the late eighteenth century and in the nineteenth (Ill. 51), sepia was so widely used as a wash that even today all other brown tones are often erroneously referred to as sepia.

In the sixteenth century indigo became more popular in the Netherlands for washing pen drawings. Its singularly cool, clear blue is produced by a strong dilution of this extract of certain tropical plants, which had long been used as a natural dye.

Chinese white, which is used for chiaroscuro drawings and to 'heighten' plastic areas of light, is usually a lead carbonate or sulphate. In the course of time this colour, which gives an opaque effect, can oxidize into brown-black.

The coloured inks, which are so familiar in miniatures (minium red) and also frequently used in drawings, have the same basic ingredients as watercolours.

Drawing Surfaces

Almost any material is suitable and in fact has been used as a drawing surface. But in artists' drawings by far the most common material used is paper in all its various forms, and only a few of the older writing materials, which were used for relatively short periods, are worth mentioning. The basic material used for writing and drawing in antiquity, papyrus, was completely superseded in the early centuries AD by parchment, which maintained its position throughout the Middle Ages. From the fourteenth century onwards, however, paper takes over entirely. Paper is a Chinese invention, generally attributed to the year AD 105; it was brought to Europe via the Near East by the Arabs. Basically it is a fibrous pulp made from mulberry bark, hemp, bast and rags, which is rolled, pressed and finally dried in a dry pulping-mould. This process has continued almost unchanged to the present time. At first, only linen rags were used in Europe as basic ingredient, but in the eighteenth century J. C. Schäffer discovered certain substitutes (vine tendrils, hops and even turf). It was not until the mid-nineteenth century, when wood-pulping began, that increased demands for paper could be met. Handmade paper, to begin with, was only 35:42 cm. in size; since the end of the eighteenth century it has been manufactured in continuous rolls. The fine lines which are visible in handmade paper when it is held against the light come from the wire screen in the mould on which wire designs can be soldered; these produce watermarks, which to this day are used as marks of origin and quality.

In earlier times the various brands of paper, like parchment and the small wooden panels, which were commonly used from antiquity until the sixteenth century, had to be specially prepared in order to guarantee a smooth, even surface for writing and drawing. This grounding continued to be essential for many drawing techniques, more particularly for silverpoint. As both the visibility and the durability of a drawing depended upon careful grounding, the artists' handbooks devote considerable space to it. The simplest grounding method was to rub in bonemeal, but other methods employed gypsum chalk, zinc or titanium white mixed with a fixative – very fine lime or gum arabic. The grounding material was applied with a broad brush in several thin coats. Too strong grounding or liming produced a brittle, fragile surface with a danger of splintering (cf. Ill. 1); too weak grounding produced a surface that was not receptive to metal, so that scratching resulted. Whereas in the north white grounding remained the most common method up to the sixteenth century, in Italy colour was added for greater effect (Plate V). From about 1400 onwards paper, as a rule, no longer required treatment, as the necessary smooth and non-absorbent surface could already be achieved in the process of production by liming the paper mass or dipping each sheet in a lime or alum bath. This also made pen drawings on paper possible. A similar smoothing effect could be achieved by applying a white or coloured coat to the paper, which at the same time performed an artistic role as a colour

ALBRECHT DÜRER
(Nuremberg 1471–1528)
The screen draughtsman.
Woodcut, *c.* 1525. 75:215 mm.
Picture of a mechanical aid to
perspective drawing. The
screen between artist and model
facilitates the two-dimensional
reproduction of the body seen
in depth

component (Plate XI). Towards the end of the fifteenth century a new kind of tinted paper emerged, the so-called natural paper or (from its place of origin) Venetian paper. This paper, usually blue in tint, remained for centuries a favourite with draughtsmen, particularly for drawings with white highlights. Grey tones, a warm light brown and flesh colours were also frequently used to colour paper. The blue paper which was originally produced only in northern Italy was introduced into Germany by Dürer and was widely used in Holland, where it was soon being produced. In consistence with the colours prevalent in painting at the time, the seventeenth century gave preference to the halftones of individual colour in their choice of drawing paper, while the eighteenth century preferred warmer colours such as ivory, beige and light brown (Plate XV). Since the nineteenth century paper of almost every colour has been used.

From the late eighteenth century onwards a distinction was drawn between paper for printing, writing or drawing. The choice of paper depended on the particular drawing technique. For the direct media even rough and absorbent paper was possible, whereas the indirect media required smooth, firm surfaces, and for pastels a firm, slightly rough ground was preferable. The absorbent 'Japanese paper' which is made from mulberry fibre, was popular as early as the seventeenth century, especially in Holland. A stronger, handmade paper with irregular edges is still known today for its high, wood-free quality. The particularly fine, grain-free vellum paper is made with a fine wire chain and has a smoothness akin to parchment. The modern watercolour paper is pure linen paper, which is limed in the mass and is free of fat or alum; the varying grain structure makes for heightened differentiation.

Aids to Drawing

Drawing is less dependent on technical aids than any other form of art and these are only employed for special purposes. Optical devices are used mainly for nature studies in order to convert the three-dimensional projection (bodies or space) more easily to the two-dimensional plane. For the purpose of depicting perspective foreshortening, the frame acquires considerable importance: the object to be drawn is seen through a rectangular network of threads, a corresponding 'screen' having been drawn on the paper; the drawing is then done over the screen (Ill. above). Until the nineteenth century portrait artists used sheets of glass on which contours and details were drawn with charcoal, chalk or even soap and then traced on the paper or directly transferred to it. Both processes play an important part in engraved reproductions of paintings. Mirrors and mirroring devices with diminishing convex mirrors or concave lenses were also employed for preliminary drawings, and sometimes for landscapes where maximum topographical accuracy was required. Similarly, in the eighteenth century the use of the highly popular *camera obscura* was in keeping with the 'objective' view of the period. Here the selected object is reflected through a lens into an oblique-angled mirror when it appears in reduced form and in reverse. To correct this a second mirror was sometimes introduced. For the purposes of transfer in the same format tracings could be made with fat-impregnated and therefore transparent paper, or with a metal or bone stylus. The marks left by these methods are usually easily discernible. A mechanical magnification or diminution can be achieved with the pantograph: the legs can be adjusted to reproduce the contours in the required scale.

145

Of the appliances for technical drawings only the compass plays some part in artists' drawings. There are also certain means of erasing which have their artistic uses, for instance in order to blur or hatch lines (Ill. 36). Correcting a drawing in drypoint was usually done with breadcrumbs until the end of the eighteenth century when the india rubber was introduced. Inks and colours which have penetrated the paper can only be removed by stronger methods – alum stone, a knife or a hard rubber.

Fixing, as a means of treating a drypoint drawing, has been known since the sixteenth century but not as a universal practice. An extremely thin coat, applied with a brush or sprayed, of a fatty, usually weak solution of lime protects the drawing against friction. The modern fixatives are heavily diluted lacquers. Unfortunately something of the immediate impact of the drawing is usually lost in the process; especially with pastels the grained surface sags and the fresh appeal of the coloured chalks becomes heavy and subdued.

Collections

Collections of hand drawings had their origin in the need of the studios for pattern drawings. In this respect they were the immediate successors to the medieval pattern-books. Most of these collections have been 'used up', destroyed or broken up and dispersed in the course of time, but various collections can be partly reconstructed from works that have survived. Other collections have remained intact, at least in essentials, examples being the Italian sheets in the Ambrosiana in Milan, and the Gentile da Fabriano and Pisanello drawings in the Codex Vallardi in the Louvre. The core of the north German drawings from the fifteenth century in the University Library at Erlangen was originally a workshop collection, probably belonging to Michael Wolgemut.

These artists' collections generally concentrate on the works of one painter, who was regarded as a model, and on his immediate environment, and, in addition to completed drawings, many studies and sketches were also preserved. In the sixteenth and seventeenth centuries this was the most common type of collection; it is still found today, though under different circumstances, in art bequests. Due to their practical purpose and basically personal nature most of these collections were dispersed after one generation or thereabouts. Where at least part of an artistic legacy was preserved for a longer period by a family, a case in point being the collection of the Buonarroti family, which was only bequeathed to the state in 1858, this was the exception rather than the rule. A more common occurrence was the preservation of a sheaf of drawings by one artist as a self-contained block, which frequently changed hands. One can, for example, trace the fortunes of a group of Leonardo drawings, which were in the possession of his pupil F. Melzi, then passed into the hands of the Spanish court sculptor P. Leone, from him to Don Juan de Espira, who sold them around 1640 to Lord Arundel, whence they finally passed to the Royal Library in Windsor Castle. The Dürer collection, which eventually found its way into the Albertina, was acquired in 1588 with great difficulty by Rudolf II, from whom it passed to Willibald Pirkheimer and the Imhoff family. Guido Reni is known to have had a portfolio of Raphael drawings and part of Carlo Maratta's collection of Dominichino's drawings is now in the Accademia de Bellas Artes in Madrid. In Rome the French painter P. Mignard acquired a sheaf of Carracci drawings, which eventually reached the Louvre by way of the Crozat and Mariette collections.

The collections of P. P. Rubens and Peter Lely, who – like Rembrandt – ruined himself in pursuit of his passion, extended far beyond any immediate or practical link with a particular workshop. Other amateurs' collections were those of Nicola Flinck, acquired by the Duke of Devonshire, and of the outstanding art collectors of the eighteenth century, including Joshua Reynolds and Thomas Lawrence. Since the nineteenth century the donation of an art collection or bequest has frequently led to local foundations. Montauban is famous for its Ingres drawings, Bayonne for the Bonnat collection; most of the Canova drawings are at Bassano and the Toulouse-Lautrec collection is at Albi – to name a few examples which demonstrate the continuing tradition of art collecting.

The didactic collections of the academies had similar origins to the artists' collections. Drawings always bulked fairly large among the teaching aids. Cartoons and sketches by famous masters were preserved at the Medici Academy of San Marco in Florence, which in the fifteenth century was the acknowledged centre of learning of the Renaissance. For teaching purposes, Cardinal F. Borromeo bequeathed his collection in 1618 to the Biblioteca Ambrosiana and the academy of painting which was attached to it. Of the academies which were established later, sometimes much later, the institutes in Paris, Madrid, Düsseldorf and Vienna still have important collections of drawings.

The first methodically assembled collection, which took account of historical associations and of the artist's personality, was that of the painter and historiographer Vasari. It was with him as model that J. v. Sandrart built up his collection. Padre S. Resta literally approached the problem from an encyclopedic point of view, when he compiled his *Galleria portatile*, one volume of which is in the Ambrosiana, another in the British Museum. The principle of cataloguing according to artist and schools became accepted in the eighteenth century, even for the major art-lovers' collections, and today it is universally applied. The first 'catalogue' was compiled by F. Baldinucci, when he arranged the splendid Medici collection of drawings.

A further category is formed by the representative collections of the secular and ecclesiastical princes who, from the sixteenth century onwards, showed increasing interest in setting up their own graphic collections. To begin with, their main interest, as is apparent from the frequent use of the term 'Kupferstichkabinett', was in prints, the reproduction of important printings. As an adjunct to the collections in museums, art galleries and libraries, collections of drawings steadily grew in numbers, but they did not receive the recognition they deserved until fairly late in the eighteenth century. Not infrequently, however, these representative collections overlapped with the interests of connoisseurs and art-lovers. To them primarily is due the high value placed on artists' drawings and the growing interest in them.

The earliest record we have is of a collection of drawings in Treviso which dates back to the fourteenth century. But it is not until the sixteenth century that specific collections and collectors' pieces can be identified. About 1530 Gabriele Vendramin in Venice was in possession of Jacopo Bellini's sketchbook, now in the British Museum, and of many Raphael drawings. A valuable collection of Holbein drawings had been assembled in the 'Kabinett Amerbach', which was purchased by the city of Basle in 1662 and now forms the nucleus of the Basle Kupferstichkabinett. But most of these private art collections were soon broken up, and even in the seventeenth century, when there was a growing interest and a lively trade in drawings, most of the collections were short-lived. A famous one was that of Charles I of England, which was put up for auction after his death; the d'Este collection, started by Alfonso III and Alfonso IV, survived until the Napoleonic wars; the Moscardo family's collection in Verona was only broken up after the first World War, when some of the drawings were acquired by the Albertina through the dealer L. Grassi *(cf. Ill. 12)*, some by the F. Lugt Collection.

The seventeenth century was also the heyday of the international art trade in drawings. The Cologne banker Eberhard Jabach twice assembled major collections, parts of which were acquired by the Louvre and the remainder auctioned in 1753. Quality was Pierre Crozat's primary motive for collecting and he paved the way for a new approach to drawing and for the connoisseurship of the late eighteenth century. Cardinal Fleury was responsible for rejecting the proposal that Crozat's collection should be acquired for the Louvre. When it was put up for auction in 1741, P. Mariette compiled the first descriptive catalogue. Mariette himself came from a family of art dealers and collectors and was an expert.

He assembled Prince Eugene's collection of engravings on which, a century later, A. Bartsch based his still definitive work *Le Peintre-Graveur*. Crozat's and Mariette's marks of ownership *(cf. Ill. p. 19)* still rank as hallmarks of quality. No less important were the contributions to collecting by Jonathan Richardson and his son in England *(cf. Ill. p. 19)*. Most of the great collections north of the Alps were started and built up in the eighteenth century. Johann F. Städel laid the foundations of the Frankfurt collection, while in Vienna Albert Casimir of Saxe-Teschen was responsible for the Albertina collection, which was on a par with the royal collections in England and Paris. Prints and drawings collections in Dresden, Munich and many other minor capitals sprang up like mushrooms; Count C. G. Tessin's important collection formed the nucleus of the Stockholm collection. Particular interest was shown in the collections of drawings in England, where, to this day, the largest number and the most impressive of private collections still exist. A fascinating personality amongst collectors was J-B. J. Wicar, who was entrusted with the task of founding a 'world museum' during the Napoleonic wars and assembled three major collections of drawings. The third, which consisted of valuable Raphael drawings, he bequeathed to his native town of Lille. Collecting in the nineteenth century and even more in the twentieth century is characterized by two extreme trends. Whereas the big collections, most of which have passed into public ownership, are scientifically assembled and slowly but surely increased, the medium-sized and small collections are highly mobile, because they are dependent on changing political and economic conditions. Within a comparatively short time individual collections come and go, while others, more particularly in America, acquire a world reputation almost overnight: examples are the Pierpoint Morgan Library, the Vanderbilt Bequest to the Metropolitan Museum in New York, the collections in Cambridge, Massachusetts, Chicago and Cleveland.

The interest of collectors in contemporary art is much stronger than it has ever been before. P. Majovszky's collection of nineteenth-century drawings, which is now in the Budapest Museum, could still be regarded as an epoch-making innovation. Today there is a direct link between artist and collector. This phenomenon may be partly attributable to the fact that fewer and fewer old drawings are available, but major collections can still be cited, such as that of F. Koenig, acquired by the Boymans-van-Beuningen Museum in Rotterdam during the Second World War, and the collections of F. Lugt in Paris and J. Scholz in New York.

Understanding of and interest in direct, individual, artistic expression, of which drawing is the finest example, are on the increase. Contemporary works are now being collected on an unprecedented scale.

Bibliography

From the abundance of books on the history and technique of drawing only those mentioned in the text together with a selection of general works can be listed.

B. Berenson, *I Disegni dei Pittori Fiorentini*, Milan 1961

W. Bernt, *Die niederländischen Zeichner des 17. Jahrhunderts*, Munich 1957/58

E. Bethe, *Buch und Bild im Altertum*, Berlin 1945

Bibliothek der Meisterzeichnungen, Hamburg 1966 ff.

K. G. Boon, *De tekenkunst in de zeventiende eeuw*, Utrecht 1955

C. Coulin, *Architekten zeichnen*, Stuttgart 1962

B. Degenhart, 'Zur Graphologie der Handzeichnung', in *Jahrbuch der Bibliotheca Hertziana* I, Vienna 1937

— *Europäische Handzeichnungen aus fünf Jahrhunderten*, Berlin–Zurich 1943

— 'Autonome Zeichnungen bei mittelalterlichen Künstlern', in *Münchner Jahrbuch der bildenden Kunst*, Munich 1950

Il Disegno Italiano [Ed. L. Grassi], Treviso 1961 ff.

O. Fischer, *Geschichte der deutschen Zeichnung und Graphik*, Munich 1951

E. Gradmann, *Spanische Meisterzeichnungen*, Frankfurt 1939

— *Bildhauerzeichnungen*, Basle 1943

L. Grassi, *Storia del Disegno*, Rome 1947

Kindlers Meisterzeichnungen aller Epochen, Zurich 1963

P. Lavallée, *Les techniques du dessin*, Paris 1949

H. Leporini, *Die Künstlerzeichnung*, Braunschweig 1955

C. Linfert, 'Die Grundlagen der Architekturzeichnung', *Kunstwissenschaftliche Forschungen I*, 1931

F. Lugt, *Les Marques de Collections de Dessin & Estampes*, Amsterdam 1921, Den Haag 1956

J. Meder, *Die Handzeichnung*, Vienna 1923

T. Mirotti, *Il collezionista di disegni*, Venice 1962

R. Oertel, 'Wandmalerei und Zeichnung in Italien. Die Anfänge der Entwurfszeichnung', in *Mitteilungen des kunsthistorischen Institutes Florenz V*, Florence 1940

G. Ring, *A Century of French Painting, 1400–1500*, London 1949

R. W. Scheller, *A Survey of Medieval Model Books*, Haarlem 1963

H. Tietze–E. Tietze-Conrat, *The Drawings of the Venetian Painters in the 15th and 16th centuries*, New York 1944

Ch. de Tolnay, *History and Technique of Old Master Drawings*, New York 1943

E. Trier, *Zeichner des 20. Jahrhunderts*, Berlin 1956

J. Watrous, *The Craft of Old-Master Drawings*, Madison 1957

M. Wheeler, *Modern Painters and Sculptors as Illustrators*, New York 1946

F. Winkler, *Die grossen Zeichner*, Berlin 1951

Monographs and Catalogues

Altdorfer F. Winzinger, *Albrecht A.s Zeichnungen*, Munich 1952

Baldung C. Koch, *Die Zeichnungen Hans B. Griens*, Berlin 1941

Bernini H. Brauer–R. Wittkower, *Die Handzeichnungen des G. L. B.*, Leipzig 1931

Bruegel L. Münz, *B. The Drawings*, London 1961

Callot D. Ternois, *Jacques C. Catalogue complet de son œuvre dessiné*, Paris 1961

Cézanne L. Venturi, *C. son art – son œuvre*, Paris 1936

Degas P. A. Lemoisne, *D. et son œuvre*, Paris 1946

Dürer H. Tietze–E. Tietze-Conrat, *Kritisches Verzeichnis der Werke Albrecht D.s*, Basle 1937

— F. Winkler, *Die Zeichnungen Albrecht D.s*, Berlin 1937–39

Dyck H. Vey, *Die Zeichnungen Van D.s*, Brussels 1962

Goltzius E. K. J. Reznicek, *Die Zeichnungen von H. G.*, Utrecht 1961

Holbein the Younger P. Ganz, *Die Handzeichnungen Hans H.s*, Berlin 1937

Koch O. Lutterotti, *J. A. K.*, Berlin 1940

Leonardo A. E. Popp, *L.s Zeichnungen*, Munich 1928

— A. E. Popham, *The Drawings of L. da Vinci*, London 1947

Michelangelo K. Frey, *Die Handzeichnungen M. Buonarrotis*, Berlin 1909–11

— L. Dussler, *Die Zeichnungen des M.*, Berlin 1959

Moore H. Read, *Henry M. Sculpture and Drawings*, London 1949

Parmigianino G. Copertini, *Il P.*, Parma 1932

Piranesi H. Thomas, *The Drawings of Giovanni Battista P.*, London 1954

Pontormo J. C. Rearich, *The Drawings of P.*, Cambridge, Mass. 1964

Poussin W. Friedlaender–A. Blunt, *The Drawings of Nicolas Poussin*, London 1939 ff.

Raphael O. Fischel, *R.s Zeichnungen*, Berlin 1913–22

Rembrandt C. Hofstede de Groot, *Die Handzeichnungen R.s*, Haarlem 1906

— O. Benesch, *The Drawings of R.*, London 1954–57

Rubens G. Glück–F. M. Haberditzl, *Die Handzeichnungen von Peter Paul R.*, Berlin 1928

— L. Burchard–R. d'Hulst, *Tekeningen van P. P. R.*, Antwerp 1956

Seurat G. Seligman, *The Drawings of Georges S.*, New York 1947

Titian D. v. Hadeln, *Zeichnungen des T.*, Berlin 1934

Troger W. Aschenbrenner–G. Schwaighofer, *Paul T.*, Salzburg 1956

Watteau K. T. Parker–J. Mathey, *Antoine W., Catalogue complet de son œuvre dessiné*, Paris 1957

British Museum. *Catalogue of British Drawings*, Vol. I., London 1960

Inventaire Général des Dessins du Musée du Louvre. 'École française.' Paris 1906 ff.

Beschreibender Katalog der Handzeichnungen in der graphischen Sammlung Albertina, Vienna 1926 ff.

Index

Arabic numerals refer to text pages; figures in italics refer to illustrations; roman numerals refer to colour plates

151

Acknowledgments

The reproductions were made with the kind permission of the museums, galleries and collections named in the captions. The publishers wish to thank the COSMOPRESS, Geneva, for permission to reproduce drawings by Picasso, Matisse and Klee.

The illustrations are taken from the following photographic agencies, museums and archives: Akademie der bildenden Künste (Kupferstichkabinett), Vienna: Plate XVI, *Ill. 50*, Ill. p. 59; Albertina, Vienna: *Ills 1*, *2*, *5*, *9*, *22*, *23*, *27*, *32*, *34*, *41*, *45*, *46*, *47*, *49*, *56*, Ills. pp. 39, 62, 133; Andover Art Studio, Andover (Mass.): *Ill. 7*; Archives Photographiques, Paris: *Ill. 16*; Art Institute, Chicago: Ills. pp. 82, 139; Ashmolean Museum, Oxford: Plate X, Ill. p. 43; Berggruen & Cie, Paris: *Ill. 55*; Joachim Blauel, Munich: Plate XIII; British Museum, London: Plate VIII, *Ill. 17*, Ill. p. 35; Cameraphoto, Venice: Plate XII; Foto A. Frequin, The Hague: Plate IX, *Ill. 10*; Gemeente Musea van Amsterdam: *Ill. 57*; Hatje Verlag, Stuttgart: Plate XIV; Foto Hinz, Basle: Plate VI; Foto Kleinhempel, Hamburg: *Ill. 28*; Royal Library, Windsor Castle: *Ill. 29*; Studios Josse Lalance & Cie, Paris: *Ills 25*, *26*, *31*, *33*, *44*, *52*; Foto Meyer, Vienna: Plates II, III; Musée Bonnat, Bayonne (Photo Marc Aubert): Plate I; Musée National du Louvre, Paris: Plate XV; National Museum of Applied Arts, Budapest: *Ill. 53*; Museum of Art, Rhode Island: *Ill. 54*; Rheinisches Bildarchiv, Cologne: *Ill. 36*; Foto Ritter, Vienna: *Ill. 12*; Foto Oscar Savio, Rome: Plate V, *Ills 6*, *13*, *14*, *15*, *43*; Schroll-Archiv: reproductions from Schroll-Albertina-Facsimile D9 (Plate IV), F 62 *(Ill. 42)*. *Ill. 4*, Ills. pp. 9, 10, 11, 15, 34, 67, 81, 83, 87, 107, 137, 138, 145; Staatliche Graphische Sammlung, Munich: *Ill. 11*; Staatliche Kunsthalle, Karlsruhe: Plate XI; Staatliche Museen, Berlin (Kupferstichkabinett): *Ill. 38*; Staatliche Museen (Nat. Gal.), Berlin: *Ill. 8*; Photo Stearn's, Cambridge (Reproduced by permission of the Syndics of the Fitzwilliam Museum, Cambridge): Plate VII; Stiftung Preussischer Kulturbesitz (Kupferstichkabinett), Berlin: *Ills 3*, *39*, *40*, *51*; Tate Gallery, London: *Ill. 37*; Uffizi (Gabinetto delle Stampe), Florence: *Ills 18*, *19*, *20*, *21*, *24*, *30*, *35*, *48*.